Language and Style in the Press

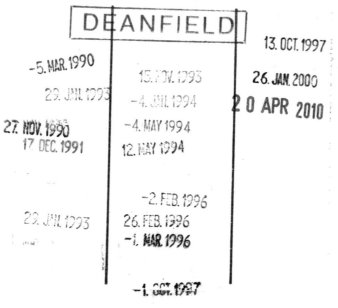

Language and Style in the Press

BARBARA DUFF
and
RAMON SHINDLER

COLLINS ELT:
London and Glasgow

Collins Educational
8 Grafton Street
London W1X 3LA

© Barbara Duff and Ramon Shindler 1984
10 9 8 7 6 5 4 3 2

First published 1984
Reprinted 1986

Designed and Typeset by Oxprint Ltd, Oxford
Printed in the Netherlands by Comproject BV Holland

Cover design by Richard Moon

ISBN 0 00 370660 5

Acknowledgements

The authors and publisher would like to thank the following for permission to
reproduce material in this book:

Associated Newspaper Group plc (for extracts from the Daily Mail and Mail on
Sunday)
The Daily Telegraph (for extracts from the Daily Telegraph and Sunday Telegraph)
The Guardian
Doug Ibbotson for 'Few Citations as Army are easily Outgunned' which originally
appeared in the Daily Telegraph (see page 72)
London Express News and Feature Services (for extracts from the Daily Express,
Sunday Express, Daily Star and The Sun)
Morning Star
The Observer
Syndication International Limited (for extracts from the Daily Mirror)
Times Newspapers Limited (for extracts from The Times and Sunday Times)

Note: Where reporters and readers are referred to as individuals and their sex is not known, the convention 's/he' is used, meaning 'he or she'.

CONTENTS

Introduction

Unit 1 Headlines

Unit 2 Reporting the news 1

Unit 3 Reporting the news 2

Unit 4 Comment

Unit 5 Reporting sport

Appendix Further suggestions for the classroom use of newspapers

INTRODUCTION

Introduction to students and teachers

This book is intended for Upper Intermediate and Advanced students of English who enjoy reading British newspapers and would like to be able to understand them better. It focuses on the language and style which often make newspapers seem difficult to a foreign learner.

There is a comprehensive answer key, which means that the book can be used for individual study. In the classroom, the exercises can also be used for pair and group work involving discussion of the articles themselves and the language contained in them.

After doing the exercises, the student should be in a better position to tackle the challenging task of reading and understanding the British Press.

The Appendix contains ideas for teachers who would like to make more use of newspapers in the classroom.

A guide to the British Press

THE DAILIES

These papers are printed and distributed on a national basis six days a week. Each one is listed below along with details of its format—whether broadsheet (39 cm × 60 cm) or tabloid (30 cm × 37 cm); its political leanings*; and a rough guide to the range of contents you might expect to find in it in any one week. The guide to contents is organised to show the relative amounts of space devoted to the various categories, those in bold type making up the bulk of the paper.

Glossary of categories

Foreign news	News from other countries, and of Britons abroad.
Home news	Political and other events which take place inside Britain and affect the nation as a whole.
Human interest stories	Stories about individuals and their lives and events that are unlikely to affect a lot of people.
Features	Articles which give background information on a country, personality or development of current interest.
Notices	Small advertisements, job advertisements, personal announcements etc.
Court and social	Official notification of the forthcoming social engagements of the Royal family, military appointments, society weddings and other similar events.
Gossip	Rumours about the private lives of prominent people.

* The political standpoints mentioned here are approximations which may vary, and are based on the authors' subjective evaluations and not offical statements from the newspapers.

THE DAILY EXPRESS (Tabloid, right of centre political standpoint.)

Commercial advertisements, human interest stories, sport, notices, home news, financial news, features, competitions and puzzles, entertainment guides, gossip, opinion and comment, reviews and previews, letters from the public, comic strips, foreign news, weather reports and forecasts, horoscopes, topical cartoons. (An average of 34 pages, about 9% pictures.)

THE DAILY MAIL (Tabloid, right of centre political standpoint.)

Commercial advertisements, sport, features, home news, human interest stories, competitions and puzzles, notices, financial news, entertainment guides, foreign news, reviews and previews, gossip, letters from the public, comic strips, opinion and comment, horoscopes, topical cartoons, parliamentary reports, weather reports and forecasts.
(An average of 36 pages, about 10% pictures.)

THE DAILY MIRROR (Tabloid, left of centre political standpoint.)

Commercial advertisements, human interest stories, sport, competitions and puzzles, home news, entertainment guides, notices, comic strips, letters from the public, features, opinion and comment, gossip, horoscopes, reviews and previews, topical cartoons, foreign news, financial news, weather reports and forecasts.
(An average of 28 pages, about 16% pictures.)

THE DAILY STAR (Tabloid, right of centre political standpoint.)

Commercial advertisements, sport, human interest stories, features, home news, entertainment guides, notices, competitions and puzzles, comic strips, opinion and comment, letters from the public, reviews and previews, horoscopes, topical cartoons, gossip, foreign news, weather reports and forecasts.
(An average of 28 pages, about 16% pictures.)

THE DAILY TELEGRAPH (Broadsheet, right of centre political standpoint.)

Commercial advertisements, notices, financial news, sport, home news, foreign news, features, entertainment guides, opinion and comment, reviews and previews, human interest stories, letters from the public, court and social, competitions and puzzles, parliamentary reports, legal reports, topical cartoons, obituaries.
(An average of 28 pages, about 5% pictures.)

FINANCIAL TIMES (Broadsheet.)

Financial news, commercial advertisements, home news, features, foreign news, notices, opinion and comment, letters from the public, entertainment, legal reports, reviews and previews, competitions and puzzles, weather, topical cartoons.
(An average of 36 pages, about 1% pictures.)

THE GUARDIAN (Broadsheet, left of centre political standpoint.)

Notices, home news, foreign news, features, commercial advertisements, financial news, sport, reviews and previews, opinion and comment, entertainment guides, letters from the public, human interest stories, topical cartoons, competitions and puzzles, weather reports and forecasts, legal reports, obituaries.
(An average of 26 pages, about 8% pictures.)

THE MORNING STAR (37 cm × 51 cm, far left political standpoint.)

Home news, sport, foreign news, features, reviews and previews, notices, entertainment guides, opinion and comment, topical cartoons, letters from the public, competitions and puzzles.
(An average of 6 pages, about 10% pictures.)

THE SUN (Tabloid, right of centre political standpoint.)

Commercial advertisements, human interest stories, sport, home news, entertainment guides, letters from the public, comic strips, opinion and comment, topical cartoons, horoscopes, foreign news.
(An average of 30 pages, about 12% pictures.)

THE TIMES (Broadsheet, centre/right of centre political standpoint.)

Financial news (including reports inserted by companies like advertisements to announce their profits etc.), **notices, features, sport, commercial advertisements, home news, foreign news, opinion and comment**, entertainment guides, reviews and previews, parliamentary reports, human interest stories, letters from the public, court and social, obituaries, weather reports and forecasts, competitions and puzzles, topical cartoons.
(An average of 26 pages, about 8% pictures.)

THE SUNDAYS

As they are produced for more relaxed Sunday reading, they differ from the dailies in that more space is given to features, comment and leisure interests.

THE MAIL ON SUNDAY (Tabloid with magazine supplement.)

NEWS OF THE WORLD (Tabloid with magazine supplement, right of centre political standpoint.) Published by the same newspaper group as *The Sun*.

THE OBSERVER (Broadsheet with magazine supplement, left of centre political standpoint.)

THE SUNDAY EXPRESS (Broadsheet with magazine supplement.)

THE SUNDAY MIRROR (Tabloid.)

THE SUNDAY PEOPLE (Tabloid, left of centre political standpoint.) Published by the same newspaper group as *The Sunday Mirror*.

THE SUNDAY TELEGRAPH (Broadsheet with magazine supplement.)

THE SUNDAY TIMES (Broadsheet with magazine supplement.)

Introduction to headlines and articles

One of the main concerns of any newspaper is to persuade the intended readers to buy copies. They will obviously buy the paper if they like what's in it. The reporter, therefore, has two important tasks.

1 To catch the attention of the reader through the *headlines* and encourage him/her to read further.
2 To hold the attention of the reader through the *articles* and encourage him/her to buy the paper again.

HEADLINES

A headline must prepare the reader for the article to follow. It must therefore be *to the point*. At the same time it must be *short* and *appeal to the attitudes and interests of the intended reader*.

MAKING A HEADLINE SHORT

1 The reporter chooses a special vocabulary.

Most of these words are commonly used in everyday English, but they are especially useful to reporters because they are particularly descriptive and/or economical.

E.g. 'soar' is more descriptive than 'rise'.
     'soar' is more economical than 'rise dramatically'.

A list of this special 'headline vocabulary' can be found on page 9. The list does not contain all the words that are ever used in headlines, but it contains all the words that are used in this book, and some of the most common ones that are not. You will be able to add to it yourself as you become more familiar with headlines.

2 The reporter uses a simplified grammar.

a *Words are left out.*

Words which do not add to the content—such as 'the', 'a' and parts of the verb 'to be'—are usually left out. In reconstructing the message, the reader may need to supply these. E.g.

Woman new Head of Bank of England = A woman is the new head of the Bank of England. (See Unit 1, Section 1, page 10.)

Actor found dead = An actor has been found dead. (See Unit 1, Section 2, page 14.)

b *Words are shortened.*

Where this is possible, abbreviations are often used. E.g.

FA angry = The Football Association is angry. (See Unit 1, Section 3, question 2, page 16.)

Doc freed = A doctor has been freed. (Unit 2, Section 5, question 7, page 35.)

c *Prepositions are avoided.* E.g.

A man from Edinburgh   ⟶ **Edinburgh man**

d *Nouns are piled in front of one another.* E.g.

A lawyer working on a case concerning ⟶ **Drugs case lawyer sacked**
drugs has been sacked   (Unit 1, Section 3, question 1, page 15.)

But there are times when nouns cannot be piled in this way and prepositions cannot be left out. E.g.

A model was killed by a doctor   ⟶ **Model killed by doctor**

A nurse was involved in a murder
incident in a village   ⟶ **Nurse in village killing**

e *Only certain verb forms are used.*

i Most verbs are in the *present simple tense*, giving the reader the sense of immediacy. E.g.

Famous actor dies means that he died very recently, probably yesterday.

ii The *simple past tense* is used for reports on reports, particularly court cases. E.g.

Lone PC fought 3 gunmen court hears —The policeman's action took place some time ago, but the court hearing has only just made it public.

This use is not very common. If you see what appears to be a past tense, it is probably the passive form with the verb 'to be' left out. (See 2a above.)

iii The *future* is usually expressed by an infinitive form with 'to'. E.g.

A Member of Parliament is going to
open a health centre   ⟶ **MP to open health centre**

But when the passive form is used in the future, the verb 'to be' is *not* left out. E.g.

Health centre to be opened by MP

Not everyone finds the same things interesting. A reporter varies the language s/he uses to appeal to the intended readership.

1 S/he can make the language s/he uses more or less descriptive or emotional.

2 S/he can make the language s/he uses more or less formal.

These points are dealt with in more detail in the section below on the articles.

3 S/he can play with the meaning or sound of the language.

1 Playing with meaning (punning).

a *Puns on words with two different meanings* where both meanings are relevant to the story. E.g.

It's the sole clue   A story where the *sole* clue to who had carried out a theft was on the *sole* of a shoe. (Unit 1, Section 5, page 18.)

b *Puns on words which are pronounced the same* but which have different spellings and different meanings. Both meanings are relevant to the story. E.g.

Weight for it!   A story where a man has to *wait* before he can collect winnings from a bet concerning his *weight*. (Unit 1, Section 6, page 20.)

c *Puns on words which have similar pronunciations* but different meanings. Both meanings are relevant to the story. E.g.

Whirl record   A story where a man sets a *world* record for flying a helicopter. *Whirl* is a reference to the motion of the helicopter's rotary blade. (Unit 1, Section 7, page 21.)

2 Playing with sound.

a *Rhyming*—words which echo each other's sound. E.g.

Greater crater   (Unit 1, Section 8, question 1, page 22.)

b *Alliteration*—words which start with the same letter or sound. E.g.

Channel champion   (Unit 1, Section 8, question 4, page 23.)

Remember—when you are looking at headlines that play with language, it is important to bear in mind that some of the connections may be rather loose.
So don't expect the precision of a dictionary. Be prepared to use your imagination.

THE ARTICLES

This book divides the articles into three different categories:

1 Those that set out to *report the news*. Any comment is indirect. (Units 2 and 3.)

2 Those that set out to *comment on the news*. (Unit 4.)

3 *Sports articles*, which are a mixture of reporting and comment. (Unit 5.)

An article must *appeal to the interests and attitudes of the intended reader*. It must also be *clear* and *economical*. (Economy is probably less important for articles which comment on the news. The reader usually has the facts already.)

APPEALING TO THE READER

1 A writer can control the style of language s/he uses.

a It can be *neutral*, *descriptive* or *emotional*. E.g.

Neutral	Descriptive	Emotional
ate	munched	
death		tragedy
fire	blaze	inferno

The style the reporter chooses will depend on the reader s/he has in mind and that reader's likely attitude to the subject matter. (Unit 2, Section 4, page 31.)

b It can be *formal/technical* or *conversational*. E.g.

Formal/technical	*Conversational*
Mr Smith	John
became interested in	took a fancy to
vaccination	jab

The style a reporter chooses will depend on the kind of relationship s/he thinks s/he should set up with the readers. If s/he wants a friendly, chatty atmosphere s/he will choose a conversational style. If s/he wants to keep some distance between writer and reader s/he will use more formal words. The choice will depend on the people s/he is writing for and the attitude s/he thinks they will have to the subject. (Unit 2, Section 5, page 34.)

2 A reporter can arrange the content of what s/he says.

a *S/he can choose the focus of the article.*
S/he can emphasise the part s/he thinks will most interest the readers, by placing it first, for example. (See also point 4 under 'Making an article clear' below.) (Unit 3, Section 2, page 40.)

b *S/he can choose which facts to cover.*
The choice will depend on what s/he thinks will be of most interest to the readers. (Unit 3, Section 3, page 42.)

3 A reporter can use humour, irony etc.

The choice depends on the readers and their likely reaction to the subject. (Unit 3, Section 5, page 46.)

4 A reporter can use literary devices.

S/he can use metaphors, adopt a dramatic style etc. Again, the decision to do this will depend on the people s/he is writing for and their likely attitude to what s/he is writing about. (Unit 2, Section 6, page 35.)

MAKING AN ARTICLE CLEAR

For an article to be clear, the ideas must be linked together. A reporter can make an article clear in the following ways:

1 The use of reference words

a The reporter can direct the reader *forwards*:
> *What* happened next was horrifying.

b The reporter can direct the reader *backwards*:
> *She* worked in a chocolate factory.

(Unit 2, Section 1, page 25.)

2 The use of linking words

E.g. *because*

'This would never work simply *because* people don't want it to.'—indicates a *reason* for a statement.

(Unit 4, Section 3, page 54.)

3 The juxtaposition of ideas

E.g.

'I didn't vote in the local elections this year. None of the candidates appealed to me.'

The second statement is the reason for the first one. (Unit 2, Section 3, question 10, page 31.)

4 The use of typography

A reporter can use CAPITAL LETTERS, *italic*, <u>underlining</u>, **bold type**; or s/he can physically arrange the printing to

- emphasise his/her points
- draw attention to his/her argument.

(Unit 4, Section 4, page 57.)

MAKING AN ARTICLE ECONOMICAL

This is less of a problem in articles which comment on the news. There is less urgency about this kind of writing.

a The reporter may use 'headline' vocabulary.

b The reporter may pile a lot of information in front of or after a noun. E.g.

Bottom-of-the-table Birmingham (Unit 5, Section 1, page 61.)	Birmingham, at present at the bottom of the league table
David Martin, the fugitive recaptured by armed police on Friday night after a dramatic chase along the London Underground, . . . (Unit 2, Section 1, question 2, page 26.)	David Martin was a fugitive. On Friday night he was recaptured by armed police. His recapture followed a chase along the London Underground.

UNIT 1
Headlines

Word list: special vocabulary

Unless otherwise indicated, these words can all be used as nouns or verbs without change of meaning.

n—only used as a noun
v—only used as a verb
c —very conversational, almost slang

	Example	*Meaning here*
aid	**£10m government aid**	assistance
alert	**Terrorist alert**	warning to be on the lookout for s.th.
axe (v)	**Council budget axed**	to dispense with
back (v)	**Tenants back Council plan**	to support
ban	**Drug ban**	prohibition
bar	**Last-minute slip bars win**	to prevent s.th. from happening
bid (n)	**Escape bid**	attempt
blast (n)	**3 die in hotel blast**	explosion
blaze (n)	**Shop blaze**	fire, usually large, out of control
blow (n)	**Blow to chances**	set-back, disappointment
boom	**Sales boom**	sudden large beneficial increase
boost	**Exports boost**	increased impetus, lift
bring (v)	**Floods bring chaos**	to cause, result in
bug (n/c)	**Bug kills babies**	disease, infection, virus
call (for)	**Better security call**	demand
clash	**Clash over Budget**	argument, conflict
cop (n/c)	**Cop in car chase drama**	policeman
crook (n/c)	**OAP's cheated by crook**	criminal
curb	**Imports curb**	restraint, restriction
cut	**Bank rate cut**	to reduce, lower
deal (n)	**Trade deal**	agreement
drama (n)	**Children in zoo drama**	dramatic action, incident
drive (n)	**Peace drive**	campaign
fear	**Assassination fear**	anxious expectation
flee (v)	**Hundreds flee famine**	to run away from s.th.
go (v)	**Church to go**	to be knocked down; sold (of property); dismantled (of institutions)
haul (n)	**Cash haul**	quantity of s.th. which has been gained, stolen, seized or gathered
hit (v)	**Snow hits sports**	to affect adversely
hold (v)	**Suspects held**	to detain in police custody
horror (n)	**Plane horror**	horrifying incident
hurdle (n)	**New hurdle to peace**	obstacle
jail	**Killer jailed**	to imprison
kid (n/c)	**Kids turn on teachers**	child
killing (n)	**Terrorist bomb killing**	incident of manslaughter, murder
link	**London arms link**	connection
loom (v)	**Strike looms**	to approach (of s.th. threatening)

9

	Example	*Meaning here*
mob (n)	**Mob attacks killer**	large gang, uncontrolled crowd
net (v)	**Police net escapees**	to capture
no (n)	**Government No to wage rise**	refusal, rejection
ordeal (n)	**Cliff-top ordeal**	unpleasant experience
peril (n)	**Flu peril**	danger
plea (n)	**Plea for blood**	strong request
pledge	**Union pledges support**	to promise
plunge	**Cliff plunge**	dramatic fall
press (v)	**MP's press for reform**	to insist on s.th.
probe	**Police probe**	investigation
quit (v)	**Director quits**	to resign, leave
quiz (v)	**Man quizzed**	to interrogate
rap	**School rap**	strong criticism, reprimand
riddle (n)	**Corpse riddle**	mystery, puzzling incident
row (n)	**Student row**	disagreement, argument
scare (n)	**Typhoid scare**	alarm (verging on panic)
seek (v)	**Flood village seeks action**	to request
shock (n)	**Rock star shock**	surprising revelation (unpleasant)
slam (v)	**Unions slammed**	to criticise severely
smash (v)	**Drugs ring smashed**	to break up, destroy
snub (v)	**Minister snubbed**	to turn down, reject (causing offence)
soar (v)	**Ticket sales soar**	to increase dramatically
storm (n)	**Government storm**	violent disagreement
threat (n)	**Drought threat**	s.th. negative which may happen
tragedy (n)	**Gun tragedy**	fatal accident, heart-breaking incident ending in death
toll (n)	**Toll rises to 100**	number of people killed
urge (v)	**PM urges inquiry**	to recommend strongly
vow	**Killer vows revenge**	to promise, threaten
wed (v)	**Actress to wed for 8th time**	to marry
win (v)	**Steel workers win rise**	to gain, achieve
woo (v)	**Tories woo householders**	to try to win the favour of

Section 1 Special vocabulary (nouns)

Before working through the exercises in this Section, you should read 'Making a headline short' on page 3 of the Introduction. You may also need to refer to the Word List on pages 9–10 for the first and last exercises.

Look at this example. This article has one *noun* missing from its headline.

The main point of the article is that a large number of people have died in the typhoon.

Look at the list that follows the articles on the page opposite. The word in the list that journalists use to refer to the number of people dead in a case like this is 'toll'.

So the headline can be completed with 'toll'.

Typhoon _____

AT LEAST 80 people were feared dead yesterday after Typhoon Bess hit central Japan causing widespread floods and landslides. Bess, which swept in from the Pacific, was downgraded yesterday as its force became spent. — Reuter.

1 Read the articles below and then complete each headline with a *noun* that makes sense from the list below.

A

JOBS _____ FOR NEW TOWN

A major oil-related company is to set up in Cumbernauld Newtown, Strathclyde, which could eventually lead to the creation of 150 jobs.

Macdonald Steel, a Buckinghamshire-based company, has taken over a 70,000 sq. ft. factory in the town's Wardpark Industrial estate to process drilling pipes for the onshore and offshore oil industry.

B

Cider _____

SALES of cider are rising faster than any other drink, according to makers Coates Gaymers. But beer consumption continues to fall, with a 12 per cent. drop in the last three years.

C

Safety _____

Tougher controls on the use of retread tyres on aircraft are urged in a Department of Trade report about an incident in which four tyres burst when a plane landed at Heathrow

D

SUGAR PAY _____

The British Sugar Corporation is to give 2,500 of its workers a 9.5 per cent pay increase despite a breakdown of talks with trade union leaders. Half the workforce had already accepted the offer, which will now be imposed on the other employees.

E

Yacht _____

LONE yachtsman Thomas Vallely, 43, of Pendlebury, near Manchester, is missing presumed drowned. Wreckage washed up near Southport has been identified as parts of his boat.

F

Press _____

ZIMBABWE's Government information department confirmed yesterday that foreign journalists would be required to inform the Government of any trips beyond 25 miles of the capital and the second largest city, Bulawayo.—AP.

G

Ski _____

TWO Dutch skiers, who were caught in an avalanche, have been rescued unharmed after spending 70 hours clinging to a tree on a ledge overhanging a 300ft drop in Vorarlberg, Austria.

H

Bangladesh _____

Brussels (AP) — The European Community granted £3.1m to Bangladesh, one of the world's poorest countries, to improve its agriculture. The grant will pay for rice and wheat seed, and for fertilizer storage centres.

I

Car _____

A BOOBYTRAPPED car exploded yesterday in front of the Iraqi Planning Ministry in Baghdad, the Iraqi news agency reported. Pedestrians and Ministry employees were killed, but no figures were given.—AP.

J

Cheese _____

TWO brothers discovered a secret hole in a warehouse wall and used it to make raids in which they stole cheese worth more than £2,000. Yesterday Peter Binney, 26, of Leeds Road, Heckmondwike, was jailed for nine months and Robert Binney, 19, of the same address, was sent to borstal.

K

£200m _____

PLANS for a £200 million sports and leisure complex at Lamesley, near Gateshead, put forward by a Texan businessman, have been thrown out following a public inquiry.

L

Big _____ for cough jabs

A CAMPAIGN to encourage parents to vaccinate their children against whooping cough is being launched following the outbreak of a national epidemic.

Last week nearly 2,000 cases were reported, 500 more than the previous week.

M

AIR RECORD _____

Two Canadian pilots took off from Montreal in a light aircraft yesterday to try to beat the around-the-world speed record.

N

Bomb _____

A LIVE 3ft. German bomb, unearthed on a building site in Altyre Road, Croydon, South London, yesterday, was carried into the site office by labourer Mick Welch—sending workmates running for cover. Army experts later took it away.

aid	blow	curb	haul	scare
bid	boom	deal	ordeal	~~toll~~
blast	boost	drive	plea	tragedy

2 Here are four phrases taken from some of the articles in exercise 1. Below them is a list of verbs.

Which verb is closest in meaning to each phrase as it is used in the article? Write your answers in the boxes.

a	take away (article N)	
b	throw out (article K)	
c	put forward (article K)	
d	take over (article A)	

acquire	display	emit	propel	reduce	remove
control	dominate	expel	propose	reject	subtract

3 Here are four verbs taken from other articles in exercise 1. Below them is a list of phrases.

Which phrase is closest in meaning to each verb as it is used in the article? Write your answers in the boxes.

a	accept (article D)	
b	discover (article J)	
c	improve (article H)	
d	explode (article I)	

blow out	build up	come over	put forward
blow up	burst out	find out	take in
bring in	come across	make up	take up

Phrasal verbs like 'put forward' and 'take over' in questions 2 and 3 above are very often used in more conversational style.

4 Below and on the next page are 12 articles and 16 headlines. Read the articles and write the appropriate headline at the top of each one. You may need to look at the Word List on pages 9–10 of this Unit.

A

A report after a three-year survey at Shipham. Somerset, where the soil and locally grown vegetables are contaminated with cadmium. has concluded that there is no evidence of a health risk.

B

EXPERTS were examining an incendiary device found early yesterday at an arson blaze at a student hostel in Bayswater Road, West London.

C

A CORONER criticised the condition of kitchens at Lancaster Moor Hospital yesterday during an inquest on five elderly patients who died from salmonella poisoning. Verdicts: Misadventure.

D

POLICE are investigating allegations that a patient at Ely mental hospital in Cardiff was ill treated. A male nurse, alleged by hospital staff to be responsible, has been suspended.

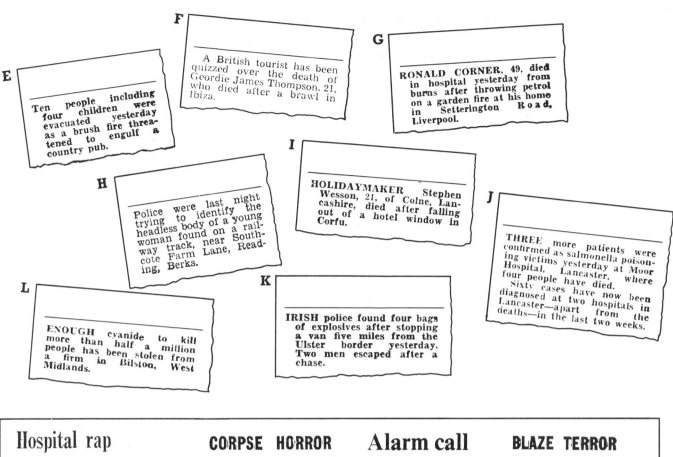

E

Ten people including four children were evacuated yesterday as a brush fire threatened to engulf a country pub.

F

A British tourist has been quizzed over the death of Geordie James Thompson, 21, who died after a brawl in Ibiza.

G

RONALD CORNER, 49, died in hospital yesterday from burns after throwing petrol on a garden fire at his home in Setterington Road, Liverpool.

H

Police were last night trying to identify the headless body of a young woman found on a railway track, near Southcote Farm Lane, Reading, Berks.

I

HOLIDAYMAKER Stephen Wesson, 21, of Colne, Lancashire, died after falling out of a hotel window in Corfu.

J

THREE more patients were confirmed as salmonella poisoning victims yesterday at Moor Hospital, Lancaster, where four people have died. Sixty cases have now been diagnosed at two hospitals in Lancaster—apart from the deaths—in the last two weeks.

K

IRISH police found four bags of explosives after stopping a van five miles from the Ulster border yesterday. Two men escaped after a chase.

L

ENOUGH cyanide to kill more than half a million people has been stolen from a firm in Bilston, West Midlands.

Hospital rap	CORPSE HORROR	Alarm call	BLAZE TERROR
Killer bug's new victims	Poison all-clear	Cruelty probe	Bomb haul
Fire-bomb riddle	Worsening toll	Blast alert	Death plunge
Poison peril	DEATH PROBE	Blaze victim	BLAZE HORROR

5 The four verbs below are taken from the articles in exercise 4. Which phrases from the list that follows are closest in meaning to each of these verbs *as they are used in the articles*? Write your answers in the boxes beside the verbs.

a	examine (article B)	
b	investigate (article D)	
c	find (article K)	
d	escape (article K)	

break out	come to	get out	look through
come across	dig up	look at	run into
come over	get away	look into	watch for

6 How would the use of these phrases in place of the verbs change the style of the articles?

Section 2 Special vocabulary (verbs) and simplified grammar

Before working through the exercise, you should read 'Making a headline short' on page 3 of the Introduction. You may also need to refer to the Word List on page 9.

Look at this example. This article has a *verb* missing from its headline.

The main point of the article is that the Editor of *The Sunday Times* is going to leave his job early.

Look at the list at the bottom of exercise 1. The verb which means the same as 'leave' is 'quit'.

Mr Giles has not left yet—he will do so in the future.

So the verb appears in the headline as 'to quit'.

Editor _____

THE Editor of The Sunday Times, Mr Frank Giles, 63, is to retire on October 1, nine months before his contract expires. He will be succeeded by 34-year-old Mr Andrew Neil, an executive on The Economist.

1 Read the articles below and then choose *ten* of the verbs from the list that follows to complete the headlines. Make sure you put the verbs in the correct form.

A

Driver _____

POLICE yesterday interviewed a tractor driver over the road death three days ago of Davina Hartburn, three, of Headingley Road, Norton, near Doncaster.

B

9,700 _____ floods

More than 9,700 people have been forced from their homes by floods in Louisiana.

C

WAITER _____

John Paterson, 34, an unemployed waiter, of St Seiriol's Road, Llandudno, was remanded in custody by Llandudno magistrates yesterday, accused of arson at the St George Hotel in the resort.

D

FIRM _____ 1,900

Littlewood chain stores and mail order empire is set to announce 1,900 redundancies. Five hundred jobs are to go at head office "JM Centre" in Liverpool and the rest at stores, offices and mail order depots across the country.

E

Cycle fares _____ by BR

BRITISH Rail is reducing many of the charges for carrying bicycles on InterCity 125 trains after complaints from cycling groups.

F

STRIKE _____ TRAVELLERS

By Our Lisbon Correspondent

A national transport strike affecting trains, ferries, buses, trams and the underground started in Portugal yesterday and was due to continue until the end of the week as trade unions demanded pay increases above the 17 per cent. ceiling established by the Government.

G

BRIDGE _____

Demolition will begin today of a 10ft 6in low railway bridge near Cwmbran, Gwent, where six passengers were killed last July when their double-deck seaside special bus hit it. The bridge has been the scene of ten other accidents in the last three years.

H

Lambeth _____ card system

The community police consultative group in Lambeth, south London, last night reversed an earlier decision to carry identity cards issued by the police. The decision concluded heated debate at three successive meetings, and was carried by 15 votes to three.

J

Building activity

The Government is expected today to announce an important concession to the construction industry when it publishes housing investment allocations for English local authorities in the coming financial year.

I

Bite _____ record

The new world record attempt for living with poisonous snakes was abandoned yesterday when John Berry, aged 21, a South African, was bitten by a young puff adder in his glass tank at Rhyl, North Wales.

axe	bar	cut	go	hold	rap	quit
ban	boost	flee	hit	loom	snub	quiz

Section 3 Simplified grammar

This Section deals with the simplified grammar of headlines. Before working through the exercises, you should read 'Making a headline short' on page 3 of the Introduction.

1 Which of the three alternatives that come after each headline is the most likely description of the contents of the article?

A

Nude woman rail killing

a A nude woman killed someone on a railway.

b A nude was killed by a woman on a railway.

c A nude woman was found killed on a railway.

B

Detectives probe new dud notes link

a Detectives are investigating a new connection in a case of forged money.

b Due to investigations detectives have uncovered more forged money.

c There is an investigation underway into a new connection between detectives and forged money.

a Someone's dying words killed a convict.

b Someone's dying words convicted a killer.

c A killer's dying words convicted him.

C

Dying words convict killer

a A father, about to become a policeman, was involved in a football incident.

b A policeman, about to become a father, was involved in a football incident.

c A policeman, who is also a father, will be involved in a football incident.

Dad-to-be PC in soccer pitch tragedy

D

E

Call for wider asbestos disease cash aid

a There has been a plea for better distribution of money to fight disease caused by asbestos.

b There has been a plea for more help to collect money to fight disease caused by asbestos.

c There has been a plea for money to help fight increasingly widespread disease caused by asbestos.

F

Terror drive cabbie jailed

a Fear sent a taxi-driver to prison.

b A taxi-driver who carried out a campaign of terror was sent to prison.

c A taxi-driver who drove dangerously was sent to prison.

G

Jab fear risk to children

a The Juvenile Advice Bureau is concerned that children are in danger.

b Fear of a particular inoculation is putting children at risk.

c There is a fear that children may be given a dangerous inoculation.

H

Workers checked after radiation leak

a Workers carried out an examination after a leak of radiation.

b Workers were questioned after an information leak about radiation.

c Workers were examined after a leak of radiation.

2 To answer question 1D you have to know that 'PC' stands for 'Police Constable'. Here are some more commonly used abbreviations. What do the letters stand for in each case? (You will probably need a dictionary to help you.)

a BBC _____   i MP _____

b BR _____   j NHS _____

c CAA _____   k PC _Police Constable_____

d CBI _____   l PT _____

e CID _____   m RSPCA _____

f EEC _____   n TUC _____

g FA _____   o UK _____

h ITV _____

Section 4 Preparing the reader for the article

The purpose of a headline is to prepare the reader for the article that will follow. This Section looks at how this is done.

1 The headline prepares a reader for the *content* of the article.

The following headlines might mislead a reader about the content of the articles. What is confusing about each one?

a **Cholera boom**   b **Death toll boost**

c **Interest rates soar by ½%**   d **Peace talks threat to new war**

e **Royal wedding looms**

2 The headline also tells the reader what sort of *style* to expect—descriptive, formal etc.

a Which of the following headlines would lead the reader to expect a more formal, technical article?

A Salmonella kills three at hospitals

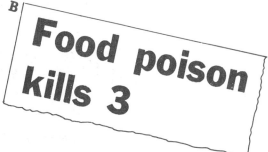

B Food poison kills 3

b According to the notes on the simplified grammar of headlines (see page 4 of the Introduction), you might expect the headlines to read:

Salmonella kills people at hospitals   **Food poison kills people**

Why is 'three' used instead of 'people'?

3 The following headlines introduce two stories on the death of a heart transplant patient. Which headline leads the reader to expect a more emotional style in the article that goes with it?

C HEART MAN DIES

D Heart tragedy

4 Which of the following headlines would lead the reader to expect a more conversational style in the article that goes with it?

E Lead risk in city grown vegetables

F 'Poison veg' warning

5 Finally, the headline prepares the reader for the reporter's *attitude* to the content.

The headlines below come from two articles on the following education story:

The Education Secretary approved the replacement of the grammar school system by the comprehensive school system in York.

Which reporter is most likely to be in favour of the Education Secretary's move?

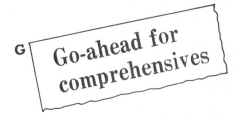

G Go-ahead for comprehensives

H SCHOOLS AXED

Section 5 Playing with language 1

This Section deals with puns involving words with two different meanings. Before working through it you should read 'Appealing to the reader' at the top of page 5 of the Introduction, and study the example below.

There is one word missing from the headline of this article. The missing word has two different meanings which are both relevant in some way to the article.

There are two clues with the article, and these should guide you to the two meanings of the missing word. The first letter of this word is given.

IT'S THE S___ CLUE

WHEN Noel Ray walked out of a store wearing a new pair of shoes, leaving his old pair on a display rack, store detectives followed him . . . because the price labels were still on the shoes he had stolen. Ray, 23, of Rutland, Freehold, Rochdale, Lancs, was fined £50 with £5 costs at Rochdale, yesterday for theft.

a Where was the price label?

b Were there other clues to the identity of the thief?

Your answers may be something like this:

a On the shoe; on the toe of the shoe; on the heel of the shoe; on the *sole* of the shoe.

b No. It was the only clue; there was only one; it was the *sole* clue.

Each question has several possible answers, but both guide you to the word 'sole'. 'Sole' is the missing word that completes the headline.

1 Read the articles below and the clues that go with them, and complete the headlines. Remember that the verbs must be in the correct form for headlines. (See the section on headlines on page 3 of the Introduction.)

A

S___, LADS!

Brothers Alan and David Smith of St Ann's, Nottingham, both have their right wrists in plaster — after breaking them in separate accidents.

a The sound of a bone breaking.

b What you might say when something you have matches what someone else has.

B

B___ it!

A MISSILE which was fired accidentally from a Danish navy frigate yesterday wrecked cottages in a Danish summer camp, but no one was hurt.

a To fire at something with heavy artillery.

b What you might say when you make a mistake.

C

Joker Steve c___ it

IRISH joker Steve Emerald wise - cracked his way to a world record yesterday.
  Steve, 40, let fly with a non-stop marathon of jokes for 30 hours at a Leeds club—and raised £350 for charity.
  Steve, of the Crossways, Otley, Yorks, said: "I reckon I got through about 8,500 gags. Now I don't want to hear another joke for a week."

a What did Steve do to the record?

b What did he do to each joke?

D

Prison r_____

There were more than 45,000 prisoners in England and Wales last year, the first time this century that the number reached that figure, the Home Office announced

a Was the number of prisoners that year the same as other years?

b What will those 45,000 criminals have when they leave prison?

2 Article C is about a man who makes people laugh by telling them jokes. Which of the following are always intended to be funny?

anecdote	recital
comment	speech
gag	wisecrack
pun	witticism

3 This exercise deals with words that have two different meanings. Each clue in the following puzzle contains two definitions. In each case the two definitions should guide you to one word.

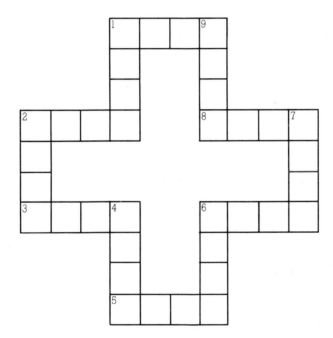

Across

1 Give out cards.
A business agreement.

2 Deposit a car.
Recreational area.

3 Roller for cotton or film.
Stagger from a blow.

5 A journey.
Cause to stumble.

6 Set of actors in a play.
Throw.

8 Signify.
Lacking in generosity.

Down

1 Common water bird.
Move down to avoid being hit.

2 Low in quality.
Having little money.

4 After all others.
To endure.

6 Device for holding papers together.
Make short or neat.

7 In good order.
Undiluted (e.g. alcohol).

9 Machine for weaving cloth.
Appear indistinctly and threateningly.

Section 6 Playing with language 2

This Section deals with puns involving words which have exactly the same pronunciation but are spelt differently and have different meanings. Both words are relevant in some way to the story. Before working through the Section, you should read 'Appealing to the reader' at the top of page 5 of the Introduction, and study the example below.

One word is missing from the headline of this article. Beside it there are two clues. The second clue should give you the missing word. The first clue should give you a word which sounds the same as the missing word but is spelt differently. This other word also has a different meaning, but it is still relevant to the article.

a Can Sidney collect the money from his friends yet?

b What is the bet based on?

Your answers may be something like this:

a No, he'll have to *wait*.

b Sidney's *weight*.

> **W___ for it!**
>
> FORMER PT instructor **S i d n e y** Barrett, 54, who weighed 14 stone last January will collect £3,000 from friends if he tips the scales at 30 stone by Christmas. He has seven pounds to go. But a doctor has warned Mr Barrett, of Trelawney Avenue, Plymouth, that he could suffer a heart attack before he collects his winnings.

The headline could have been **Wait for it!**

But for effect, the reporter replaced the word 'wait' with the word 'weight'. The headline still sounds the same, but now it has a double meaning: (**Weight**) for it!

1 Read the articles below and the clues that go with them, and then complete the headlines.

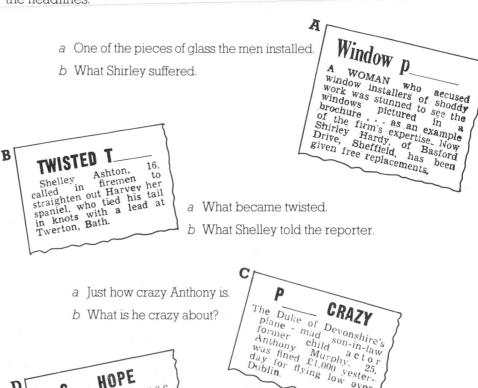

a One of the pieces of glass the men installed.

b What Shirley suffered.

> **A**
>
> **Window p___**
>
> A WOMAN who accused window installers of shoddy work was stunned to see the windows pictured in a brochure ... as an example of the firm's expertise. Now Shirley Hardy, of Basford Drive, Sheffield, has been given free replacements.

> **B**
>
> **TWISTED T___**
>
> Shelley Ashton, 16, called in firemen to straighten out Harvey her spaniel, who tied his tail in knots with a lead at Twerton, Bath.

a What became twisted.

b What Shelley told the reporter.

a Just how crazy Anthony is.

b What is he crazy about?

> **C**
>
> **P___ CRAZY**
>
> The Duke of Devonshire's plane - mad son-in-law former child actor Anthony Murphy, 25, was fined £1,000 yesterday for flying low over Dublin.

> **D**
>
> **S___ HOPE**
>
> Psychologist George Kiss has won a £27,000 grant to programme a computer at Warwick University to "feel" emotion and "fall in love."

a How much hope is there of George succeeding?

b £27,000 is quite a large one!

2 This exercise deals with words which are pronounced the same but have different spellings and meanings. The clues to the puzzle below are grouped in pairs. Each pair should guide you to two words with the same pronunciation.

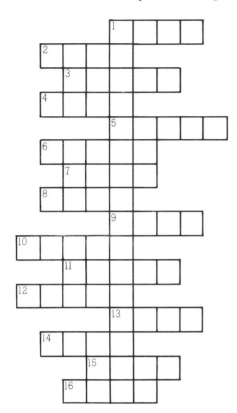

Across

1 Female servant.
2 Constructed.

3 Perfume.
4 Transmitted.

5 Person under age.
6 He works in a pit.

7 Achievement.
8 You stand on them.

9 One of 18 in golf.
10 Complete.

11 Take what's not yours.
12 Hard alloy used for knives.

13 Found on head and body.
14 Fast animal, like a rabbit.

15 It catches the wind to move a boat.
16 Exchange of goods for money.

Down

1 Come face to face with.
5 Flesh of animal, used as food.

9 Back part of human foot.
13 Make healthy again.

Section 7 Playing with language 3

This Section deals with puns involving words with a *similar* pronunciation but different spellings and meanings. Both words are relevant in some way to the story. Before working through the exercise, you should read 'Appealing to the reader' at the top of page 5 of the Introduction, and study the example below.

This article's headline looks rather unusual. Look at the word which is underlined. Although 'whirl' is relevant to the story, it has been put into the headline mainly to make you think of another word. This other word sounds similar to 'whirl', and its meaning is also relevant to the story. If it replaced 'whirl', it would produce a more normal-looking headline with no double meaning.

There are two clues beside the article. The first should help you to see how the headline is relevant to the story. The second should help you to find the other word.

a What do the blades on Ross's aircraft do?

b Has Ross's performance been bettered anywhere else?

The other word is: _____

Whirl record

TEXAN Ross Perot, 23, has become the first man to fly round the world in a helicopter. He took a month.

Your answers may be something like this:

a Go round; spin; revolve; *whirl.*

b No, he's the first man in the world to do it. It's a *world* record.

'World' sounds similar to 'whirl'. It is relevant to the story. **World record** would make a more normal-looking headline without a double meaning. 'Whirl' has been chosen to make you think of 'world'.

1 The headlines to the following articles all make use of the same effect. Read the articles and the clues and find the 'other word' in each case.

A

> **Yappy ending**
> THE barking of Rex, a mongrel who started life as an unwanted puppy, yesterday saved a family of five from their blazing home in Nottingham.

a How you might describe a small dog that makes a lot of noise.

b Was the result of the fire a tragedy?

The other word is: _____

a To defreeze.

b How you might describe a bone of contention such as this.

The other word is: _____

B

> **THAW POINT**
> A California firm who deep-freeze bodies to preserve them for the future are threatening to thaw out an old couple because of unpaid fees.

C

> **L of a wait**
> THE national average waiting time for a driving test is 13 weeks, Junior Transport Minister Lynda Checker disclosed yesterday.

a What the people who are waiting for a driving test must display on their cars in the meantime.

b A very long wait.

The other word is: _____

a The sound made by that kind of animal.

b The bad deal he got from the situation.

The other word is: _____

D

> **ROAR DEAL**
> Farmer Alex Rough landed his crippled helicopter safely in South Africa's Transvaal game park . . . only to find himself surrounded by lions

Section 8 Playing with language 4

This Section deals with headlines that depend on sound for their effect. Before working through the exercise, you should read 'Appealing to the reader' at the top of page 5 of the Introduction, and study the example below.

Look at this example. The article has a two-word headline, but one of the words is missing. There is only one clue to help you find the missing word, but it rhymes with the other word.

> **Greater** _____
> AN underground atomic blast caused a cave-in under the Navada Desert big enough to swallow a skyscraper, a US Energy Department spokesman said yesterday.

Clue: What appeared in the Nevada desert after the blast.

The missing word *refers to* what appeared in the Nevada desert after the blast, and *rhymes with* 'Greater'.

Answer: crater.

1 Complete the headlines below.

Clue: One of what Eddie is trying to find.

A

> _____ **Venture**
> Holidaymaker Eddie Beard 56, yesterday offered a £5 reward for the return of his false teeth . . . which he lost surfing at Sandbanks, Dorset.

Clue: The result of lifting things that are too heavy.

B
Crane _____

A SPECIAL study into stress involved in operating cranes — particularly those on construction sites — has been commissioned by an insurance company.

Clue: The part of the butterfly that probably set off the alarm.

C
_____ **ding**

THE mystery cause of a burglar alarm repeatedly going off at Culverhay School. Bath, has been found to be a Red Admiral butterfly which crawled inside as a caterpillar. It has been freed.

2 Article C is about the mystery of why an alarm bell kept 'going off' or sounding.

Here is a list of other phrases using the verb 'go':

| go against | go for | go off | go on | go over |

Choose one of these phrases from the list and put it in the correct form to complete each of the sentences below. The phrase should mean the same as the word in the box in each case.

a	The bomb _____ and the whole building blew up.	exploded
b	He _____ his father's orders and sold the house.	disobeyed
c	When he _____ the figures he found some basic errors.	checked
d	The wound healed in a week, but the pain _____ for months afterwards.	continued
e	The dog always _____ the postman.	attacked

3 What effect would the use of the verbs rather than the phrases have on the style of these five sentences?

Look at this example. This article has a two-word headline, but one of the words is partly missing. There is a clue to help you find the missing word. This time it begins with the same sound as the other word.

Clue: What Mike has been able to call himself since he broke the record.

Channel Ch _____

MIKE READ, 41, from Ipswich, has made his 24th successful Channel swim, nine times more than any other swimmer. He took 12 hours 54 minutes from the beach at Dover to France.

The missing word refers to what Mike can now call himself, and it starts with the sound 'ch . . . .'.

Answer: (champion)

4 Complete the following headlines. (You will probably need a dictionary.)

Clue: The kind of blow Matthew might give an opponent.

A

CHARITY CH___

Exhibitions by karate kid Matthew Treharne, 10, of Bretton, near Peterborough. Britain's youngest black belt, have raised £3,000 for charity.

Clue: Another word for the hitch Sid caused.

B

Snake sn___

POISONOUS catseye snake Sid bought to guard £1,000 worth of Silver on exhibit at Carlisle Art Gallery has been "sacked". He turned out to be nocturnal, only coming awake when all the visitors had left.

Clue: The kind of situation the teacher found herself in.

C

Quads qua___

THE four-year-old Nowakowski quads — Andrej, Marek, Janusz and Stefan — posed a problem for the teacher when they started school at Woodthorpe, Nottinghamshire, yesterday. She couldn't tell which was which.

5 Article B says that Sid 'turned out to be nocturnal'. What does this mean?

a He had always been nocturnal, but no-one at the Gallery knew it.

b He suddenly became nocturnal at the Gallery.

c He had been trained to be nocturnal.

6 In each of the following sentences there is a phrase containing the verb 'turn'. From the list below, choose one word or expression which means the same as the phrase as it is used in each sentence. Write your answers in the boxes.

a They were so tired that they *turned in* for the night.	
b The offer was so poor that they *turned* it *down*.	
c They *turned up* late for the appointment.	
d When he ran out of money he *turned to* me for help.	
e As the cinema was full, we were *turned away*.	

approached	departed	refused entry	retired
arrived	disappointed	rejected	telephoned
cancelled their plans	ignored		

7 What effect does the use of the phrases rather than the verbs have on the style of these five sentences?

UNIT 2
Reporting the news 1

Section 1 Making reporting clear and economical

This Section looks at how reporters try to make their writing clear and economical.

1 Look at the articles below. They both concern the same news incident.

A

Tourists die in cable-car plunge

SINGAPORE: A floating oil rig struck two cable-cars over Singapore harbour on Saturday, throwing seven tourists to their deaths and trapping 13 others in cars swinging 100 feet above the water.

Jokes in the cable car trap

SINGAPORE

THE 13 survivors of the Singapore cable car tragedy told jokes to keep from panicking as they waited all night to be rescued, it was revealed yesterday.

B

a Which is the 'first report' of the incident and which assumes that the readers have read the main points already?

b What gave you your answer?

When the new information is introduced for the first time in extract A, it appears as

> 'A floating oil rig'
> 'two cable-cars'
> 'seven tourists'

'*Their* deaths' and '*others*', which appear later, are references to the tourists already mentioned.

Extract B, however, starts by referring to '*the* 13 survivors' and '*the* Singapore cable car tragedy'. The reporter assumes that the reader knows which survivors and which tragedy s/he is writing about. They were probably mentioned in an earlier article.

This kind of reference to people, things and ideas already mentioned is important in understanding all kinds of English.

2 The following extracts concern different stages of a single news story. In extract C, the reporter describes Stephen Waldorf as the 'wrong man shooting victim'. This summary reminds the reader of what has already happened. The reporter can then go on to the next piece of news. 'Wrong man shooting victim' is a summary of an earlier incident.

Look at the other extracts. Where is this incident first reported?

C
WRONG MAN shooting victim Steven Waldorf was allowed to dress and take a short walk in hospital yesterday as his recovery continued.

Steven, 25, gunned down in a car in London's Earls Court after being mistaken for Britain's most wanted man, David Martin, also read about himself in the newspapers for the first time since the accident 11 days ago.

D
DAVID MARTIN, the fugitive recaptured by armed police on Friday night after a dramatic chase along the London Underground, was last night charged with two fresh offences alleged to involve property worth more than £26,000.

F
IN a frightening and alien scene to Britain, a squad of police gunmen ambushed a car in the London rush hour last night and pumped seven bullets into the driver.

They thought he was David Martin, a dangerous escaped prisoner. But they had the wrong man. A completely innocent man, 26-year-old film editor Stephen Waldorf.

E
A POLICE OFFICER was charged with attempted murder last night in the "wrong-man" shooting of Stephen Waldorf.*

G
THE two London detectives charged as a result of the shooting of Stephen Waldorf last week were released on unconditional bail on the advice of the Director of Public Prosecutions yesterday.

H
THE five-week hunt for David Martin ended last night when the 35-year-old fugitive was arrested by armed Flying Squad detectives after being chased for nearly a mile through a tunnel in the London Underground.

I
POLICE hunting an escaped prisoner accused of attempting to murder a constable warned the public last night : "Don't have a go."

They fear David Martin, 35, may have got hold of guns after breaking out of London's Marlborough Street court on Christmas Eve.

Said Detective Superintendent George Ness :

"This man is very violent.

"Members of the public are asked not to approach him, but to inform the police immediately."

J
THREE detectives involved in the Kensington ambush were suspended from duty last night.

One is a constable from D District and the others are constables from the Yard's criminal intelligence branch, C11.

A spokesman said: 'They have been suspended pending the result of the inquiry or until further notice'.

* The officer was later aquitted.

3 The form of the summary in extract C is typical of newspaper style. As with headlines, the nouns and adjectives are piled in front of the noun so that a lot of information can be contained in a small space. This is economical.

Rewrite the first sentence of extract C as it might be if the writer didn't have to worry about being economical.

4 The first three lines of extract D refer to an earlier incident. In which extract was the incident reported for the first time?

5 In the fourth line of extract D, the reporter mentions 'two fresh offences'. What information does this give you about the past?

6 The extracts were not printed in the order that they are presented here. Put the letters of the extracts in the table below to show their correct order. To help you, use the kind of reference clues that have already been mentioned:

reference words (such as 'the' etc.)
words which contain a reference in their meaning (such as 'fresh')
summary references to earlier incidents

1	2	3	4	5	6	7	8

7 Look at the beginning of this article:

K

Ringing up those wedding bells...

WHEN St Valentine's Day comes (next Monday), can wedding bells be far behind ?

Barclays Bank favours young lovers, for how otherwise will it find customers for its Getting Married account ?

With a nice blend of commercialism and the romantic, the bank runs this special regular savings scheme for young couples with a year-long engagement ahead.

Both parties agree to open

The reporter writes about '*those* wedding bells'. Which of the following do you think 'those' refers to?

a The wedding bells the reader is going to learn about in the article.

b The wedding bells the reader learnt about in an earlier article.

c The wedding bells the reader knows about from his everyday life.

8 What difference does the word 'up' make to the headline of extract K?

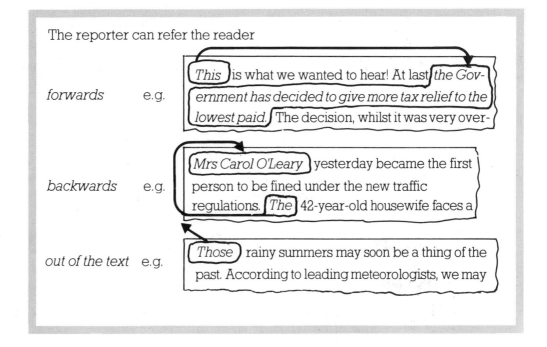

The reporter can refer the reader

forwards e.g. *This* is what we wanted to hear! At last *the Government has decided to give more tax relief to the lowest paid.* The decision, whilst it was very over–

backwards e.g. *Mrs Carol O'Leary* yesterday became the first person to be fined under the new traffic regulations. *The* 42-year-old housewife faces a

out of the text e.g. *Those* rainy summers may soon be a thing of the past. According to leading meteorologists, we may

Section 2 Making reporting interesting

This Section deals with reference in a complete article.

A

The night the heavy mob* came to call

A BULL in a china shop is legend. This story is fact—reported yesterday by a major insurance company.

* The phrase 'the heavy mob' comes from gangster terminology. It usually refers to a gang of muscle-men who visit a victim to put pressure on him with the threat or use of violence.

1   It is quite common in conversational English to describe someone as 'like a bull in a china shop'. What sort of person would this refer to?

   a Someone whose movements are always careful.

   b A clumsy person with a tendency to break things.

   c Someone who buys a lot of unnecessary things.

2   Why does the reporter compare what happened in the story with the idea of a bull in a china shop?

   a Because it is similar in some ways to the idea of a bull in a china shop.

   b Because, unlike the story of the bull in a china shop, the news story happened recently.

   c Because the idea of a bull in a china shop is more believable than this news story.

3   From the information contained in the headline and the first paragraph, what is the article most likely to be about?

   a A visit by some animals which led to an insurance claim for damages.

   b A visit which resulted in the insurance of some famous china.

   c A visit by some gangsters to an insurance company.

   d None of these.

4   The rest of the article follows below, but the paragraphs are not in the correct order. Complete the table to show their correct order. Remember to look for the kind of reference clues mentioned in Section 1.

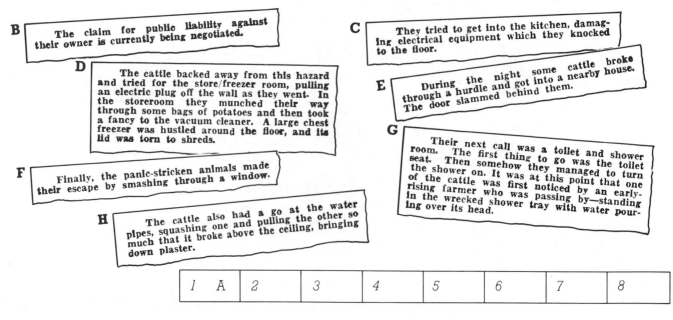

B The claim for public liability against their owner is currently being negotiated.

C They tried to get into the kitchen, damaging electrical equipment which they knocked to the floor.

D The cattle backed away from this hazard and tried for the store/freezer room, pulling an electric plug off the wall as they went. In the storeroom they munched their way through some bags of potatoes and then took a fancy to the vacuum cleaner. A large chest freezer was hustled around the floor, and its lid was torn to shreds.

E During the night some cattle broke through a hurdle and got into a nearby house. The door slammed behind them.

F Finally, the panic-stricken animals made their escape by smashing through a window.

G Their next call was a toilet and shower room. The first thing to go was the toilet seat. Then somehow they managed to turn the shower on. It was at this point that one of the cattle was first noticed by an early-rising farmer who was passing by—standing in the wrecked shower tray with water pouring over its head.

H The cattle also had a go at the water pipes, squashing one and pulling the other so much that it broke above the ceiling, bringing down plaster.

1	A	2		3		4		5		6		7		8	

Throughout the article the following references are made to the cattle:

The cattle, the panic-stricken animals, they, their, them

Notice how these are varied to keep the article interesting.

5   The reporter has also tried to make his/her writing more interesting by choosing descriptive rather than neutral language. This is why, for example, s/he uses 'munched' instead of 'ate' in paragraph D.

Which descriptive words does s/he use instead of the following:

push (paragraph D)	
shut (paragraph E)	
break (paragraph F)	

6   The reporter has also adopted a conversational style. This is why s/he uses 'took a fancy to' in paragraph D instead of the more formal 'became interested in'. Which conversational phrase does s/he use instead of the following:

attack (paragraph H)	

7   You can see now that the story is not about gangsters. Why do you think the reporter included a piece of gangster slang—'the heavy mob'—in the headline?

8a As you saw in question 5, 'munched' is more descriptive than 'ate'. To 'munch' is to eat with a lot of jaw movement and obvious enjoyment.

The list below contains descriptive words that add more to the ideas of eating or drinking. Complete the table to show whether the words refer to eating, drinking or both.

bolt	crunch	gnaw	gulp	nibble	slurp
chew	down	gobble	~~munch~~	sip	swig

Eating	Drinking
munch	

b   What does each verb add to the idea of eating or drinking? (Use a dictionary to help you if necessary.)

Section 3 Consolidation

This Section brings together the points already made in this Unit.

Visitor sets bird-watchers a flutter

By a Staff Reporter

Hundreds of ornithologists crept on to mudflats on Seal Sands at the mouth of the river Tees yesterday for a glimpse of one of Britain's rarest feathered visitors.

The bird is "98 per cent certain" to be a long-toed stint, a member of the sandpiper family, according to the Royal Society for the Protection of Birds. Normally, it nests in Siberia and winters in south-east Asia, sometimes reaching Australia.

The last confirmed sighting west of Siberia was in Sweden five years ago. A reported sighting in Cornwall 12 years ago has still not been officially accepted. But now the 6-inch chestnut and white wader with distinctive white eyebrows and abnormally long feet has some-how joined the thousands of birds on the Tees estuary bird sanctuary — with timing which has delighted conservationists.

It was first sighted by Mr John Dunnett, of Thornaby, on Saturday — the day after Stockton Council had discussed in secret a plan by Phillips Petroleum to dump oil waste from the Ekofisk field in the North Sea at five one-acre sites adjoining the estuary reserve.

Stockton council has decided to seek more evidence on the ornithological importance of Seal Sands before making any final decision on Phillips's application.

---

1   Look at the headline to the report above.

   To 'set someone a-flutter' is a more conversational way of saying to 'excite' them. Why is 'sets . . . a-flutter' particularly effective in this context?

2   Why is 'bird-watchers' more suitable than 'ornithologists' for this particular headline?

3   Which of the following means the same as 'crept' (line 2)?

   a moved quickly and noisily
   b moved quickly but quietly
   c moved slowly and quietly

4   What do you expect 'mudflats' (line 2) to be?

   a a kind of boat
   b a kind of house
   c a kind of land

5   Which sense do you expect 'glimpse' (line 5) to be connected with?

   a sight
   b sound
   c touch

Look at line 7. The writer has used inverted commas around ' "98 per cent certain" '. Inverted commas are most commonly used to indicate some kind of quotation, normally of one of the following.

   a A well-known saying.

   b Someone else's words.

   c The title of a book, film, competition etc.

---

6   Which of the three types of quotation in the box above is the writer recording in line 7?

7a The 'mouth of the river Tees' is mentioned for the first time in lines 3–4. It is mentioned again later, but to make it more interesting, different words are used. Circle this second reference.

b The article is about a bird, but the word 'bird' is only used once (line 7). Underline all the other ways the bird is referred to in the article.

8   Look at lines 21–27. The reporter wants to give a lot of detail as economically as possible. S/he has added extra information to the basic facts by piling ideas before and after them.

   Rewrite the description of the bird (lines 21–24) in separate sentences as it might be written if the reporter didn't have to use an economical style.

9 Pick out the basic facts from this sentence and write a headline which is as short as possible.

10 Which of the following is the best illustration of the relationship between what comes before and after the dashes in lines 27 and 31?

  a STATEMENT — plus EXAMPLE

  b STATEMENT — plus CONTRAST

  c STATEMENT — plus ADDITIONAL INFORMATION

11 Why has the bird's timing 'delighted conservationists' (line 28)?

  a Because hundreds of ornithologists were there to see it.
  b Because it coincided with a petroleum company's request to dump rubbish there.
  c Because the last sighting of this breed of bird in Britain was 12 years ago.

12 According to the last paragraph (lines 38–43), Stockton Council has not yet made a decision on Phillips's application.

  Which of the following is most likely?

  a The arrival of the bird will encourage the Council to say 'No' to Phillips.
  b The arrival of the bird will encourage the Council to say 'Yes' to Phillips.
  c The arrival of the bird will have no effect on their decision.

13 The words 'ornithologists' and 'bird-watchers' both refer to the same group of people, but 'ornithologist' is a more formal, technical term.

  The list below contains pairs of words like this. Complete the table by matching the pairs with the same meanings and then deciding which of the two is more technical in each case. (You may need to use a dictionary.)

		Technical
astronaut bird-watcher cartographer eye specialist map-maker meteorologist misogynist ophthalmologist ornithologist space-man weather-man woman-hater	bird-watcher	ornithologist

Section 4 Appealing to the interests and attitudes of the reader

This Section looks at how reporters choose language to make their stories appeal to the interests and attitudes of their readers.

1 Look at these headlines.

A 'Hidden workforce' of 1.5m children

B SCANDAL OF 'SLAVE' KIDS

The table below compares the attitudes of the two writers to the child workforce. Using the headlines to make your decision, tick the appropriate spaces in the table.

	The writer thinks the child workforce:		It is impossible to tell what s/he thinks of it.
	is a good thing	is a bad thing	
Headline A			
Headline B			

2 What language in the headlines gave you your answer?

3 The first paragraph of each of the articles follows. Match the articles to the headlines.

C
UP TO £1½million children could be adding to Britain's unemployment problem by doing illegal jobs. A shock survey says the children are being used as cheap labour in building sites, fairgrounds and street markets.

D
The Low Pay Unit says that Britain could have a hidden workforce of up to 1.5 million children, many of them working long hours for less than £1 an hour.

The headlines of both articles use inverted commas.

In Section 3 you saw inverted commas used to indicate quotations.

Inverted commas can also draw the reader's attention to the fact that the style of one particular word or phrase is different from that of the rest of the passage. The difference could be in the shape of any of the following:

a piece of slang or a technical term in otherwise standard English

irony, pun or metaphor in an otherwise literal passage

the writer's idiosyncratic use of a word

4 Look at the inverted commas in the headlines.

A 'Hidden workforce' **B** 'SLAVE'

Decide which of the following reasons for the use of inverted commas applies to each of the headlines. Then write the letters of the headlines in the appropriate spaces.

Reasons (quotations)	Letter
a Quoting a well-known saying.	
b Quoting someone else's words.	
c Quoting the title of a book, film, competition etc.	

Reasons (unusual use of the language)	Letter
d Drawing attention to the use of irony.	
e Drawing attention to the writer's use of a nickname or special term for something.	
f Drawing attention to the use of a technical term in a non-technical article.	

5 Here are two versions of the same article. The one on the left has been changed. The words the reporter chose to make his/her story interesting have been left out or replaced by the words in italic. The reporter's original words are in the box at the bottom. Complete the report on the right by putting the reporter's original words into the correct places.

Version 1

Over 100 police *descended* on Brixton yesterday and used axes to break into houses and commercial buildings. Local people said that 11 homes had been 'devastated'.

This show of force took place in Railton Road—the 'Front Line'. Seven people were arrested.

The atmosphere there last night was *changeable* as *angry* black people gathered to see the damage done.

In one instance, police, apparently wearing riot headgear, *went* into a private house and *took* a mattress off the bed on which five-month-old baby Marly was sleeping.

Martin Thomas, asleep near to the baby in the upstairs bedroom was *pulled* off the bed and then the police, *carrying* iron bars, *cut* open the mattress and broke down cupboard and wardrobe doors.

Version 2

Over 100 police *a* ____ on *b* ____ Brixton yesterday and used axes to break into houses and commercial buildings. Local people said that 11 homes had been 'devastated'.

This *c* ____ show of *d* ____ force took place in Railton Road—the 'Front Line'. Seven people were arrested.

The atmosphere there last night was *e* ____ as *f* ____ black people gathered to see the damage done.

In one instance, police, apparently wearing riot headgear, *g* ____ into a private house and *h* ____ a mattress off the bed on which five-month-old baby Marly was sleeping.

Martin Thomas, asleep near to the baby in the upstairs bedroom was *i* ____ off the bed and then the police, *j* ____ iron bars, *k* ____ open the mattress and broke down cupboard and wardrobe doors.

Original words

armed with	dragged	provocative	stormed
battered	dragged	slashed	volatile
brutal	incensed	swooped	

6 What attitude does the reporter expect his/her readers to have towards the police and their visit?

Which words tell you about the writer's attitude?

7 Which of the following sentences could have come later in the original article?

a A similar thing happened next door when police went into a temple and took some wood panels off the walls.

b It was the same story of mindless violence all over Brixton until the police finally managed to round up the brutal troublemakers.

c Here it was the same scene of senseless havoc with drawers tipped out of cabinets and their contents strewn around the floor.

Whenever a writer chooses *emotional* rather than *neutral* language, s/he is expressing an attitude.

If a writer chooses a lot of emotional language his/her writing may eventually have more in common with subjective *comment* than with objective *reporting*.

Section 5 Degrees of formality in reporting

In addition to the variations mentioned in Section 4, this Section looks at how the relationship between the reader and the reporter depends on the choice of formal or conversational language.

1 The following extracts are the opening paragraphs from two different reports on the same incident.

A
A football referee was assaulted by five members of a family whose team had just lost a match by 6-1 in November last year, a court was told yesterday.

B
FIVE members of a soccer-mad family ganged up on the referee after their team was thrashed 6—1.

Complete the table below with quotations from the articles to show the contrast between the two.

	Descriptive and conversational	Formal and neutral
Language concerning the attack	(Article)	(Article)
Language concerning the score	(Article)	(Article)

2 Here are the headlines from the two articles.

C
Family kick the referee

D
SOCCER FAMILY PUT BOOT IN ON THE REF

According to 'Making a headline short' on page 3 of the Introduction, words like 'the' are normally left out of headlines. Why do you think that 'the' is included in both of these headlines?

3 Match the headlines to the articles.

> In the case of articles A and B, the reporter who created a more formal relationship with the readers also used more neutral language. Perhaps s/he felt that a descriptive, conversational report of such a serious event would not seem appropriate. In choosing his/her style, a reporter has to take into account the subject matter and how the readers are likely to react to it.

4 Look at the following headlines. Which one was written by a reporter who thinks that a lighthearted, conversational approach is appropriate?

E
Phone help for heart victims

F
DIAL A HEART SAVER!

5 Each headline has three accompanying paragraphs. Match the paragraphs below to the headlines.

G Callers who dial 999 are told how to give mouth-to mouth resuscitation until an ambulance crew arrives. The advice is given by a telephone operator at an ambulance station, reading from a script.

H Callers dialling 999 for an ambulance will be handed over to an operator who will tell them how they can keep the patient alive until help arrives.

I A SPEAKING-DOC phone-in service was launched yesterday in a bid to save the lives of heart attack victims.

J The idea comes from Seattle, in the United States, where it increased the survival rate of heart victims. It can also help with drug overdoses.

K The scheme being launched in Avon, was pioneered in America where it trebled the survival rate.

L A telephone service to enable untrained people to help heart attack victims was launched in Avon yesterday.

6 The headlines below come from two articles about a robber who confessed at his trial that he was guilty and promised that he was finished with crime for ever.

M Raider's remorse fails to stop 10 years jail

N Never again vows crook

What makes headline N more conversational?

7 Headline C (see question 2) referred to the 'referee', while headline D called him the 'ref'. It is quite common for abbreviations like this to appear in newspapers, especially headlines. What are the following abbreviations short for?

a	ad	_____	f rep	_____
b	doc	_____	g rev	_____
c	hubby	_____	h veg	_____
d	lab	_____	i vet	_____
e	ref	*referee*	j welly	_____

Section 6 Subject matter and the style of reporting

This Section looks at the way two different reporters deal with a less serious subject. Read this article and answer the questions that follow.

A

DRIVER WRECKS HIS OWN CAR

A frustrated motorist who had just had his F registered car repaired could take no more when it broke down on
5 the M5 near Stroud, Gloucester, yesterday. His anger boiled over and he decided to put it out of its misery.

Snatching a sledge-hammer
10 from the boot he attacked the car, smashing the windows and raining blows on the bodywork. Curious police officers who went to investigate said the
15 driver, from Cheltenham, Glos, had committed no offence.

1   The phrase 'could take no more' (lines 3–4) sounds more dramatic than 'got fed up'. In view of the subject matter, what is the effect of using such a dramatic style here?

2   Words like 'erupted' and 'exploded' would probably fit into the dramatic style better than 'boiled over'. Why, then, does the reporter choose to say that the man's anger 'boiled over' in lines 6–7?

3   What would you normally 'put out of its misery' (lines 7–8)?

4   What would be the effect of using 'taking' instead of 'snatching' in line 9?

5   Rewrite the following phrases to make them less descriptive:

'smashing the windows' (line 11)
'raining blows' (line 12)

6   Look at your answers to the questions above. What sort of reaction does the reporter expect from his/her readers?

   a amusement
   b concern
   c shock

7a   According to 'Making a headline short' on page 3 of the Introduction, unnecessary words are usually left out of headlines. In view of this, why didn't the reporter choose the headline **Driver wrecks car**?

 b   Why didn't s/he choose **Driver wrecks his car** or **Driver wrecks own car**?

8   Here is a second report on the same incident.

B

A BANGER GETS THE HAMMER

A MYSTERY driver turned a motorway hard - shoulder into a scrap - yard yesterday.

He stormed out of his car after it broke down.

Passing motorists gaped in amazement as he waded into it . . . with a sledge-hammer.

He started on the wind-screen and caved in all the windows before switch-ing his attention to the bodywork.

A few hefty blows reduced the F registered Rover to a crumpled heap.

Then the driver walked over to an emergency phone and made arrange-ments for the wreckage to be towed to a breaker's yard.

Police went to the scene of the car-nage on the M5 near Stroud, Gloucester-shire.

But they decided the only thing the wrecker hadn't broken was the law.

Police later refused to name the driver, who comes from Cheltenham.

But a spokesman said: "He had just had the car repaired and it appears he lost his temper when it broke down again."

What effect does the reporter get by writing about a 'mystery driver' (line 1) instead of an 'unidentified driver', or an 'unnamed driver'?

9   In article B the reporter writes that the motorway hard shoulder was turned into a 'scrap-yard' (line 4). How would you describe this phrase?

   a An accurate description.
   b An exaggerated description.
   c An understatement.

10   Why do you think the driver 'stormed' out of his car in line 6, but 'walked' over to the phone in line 20?

11   Write 'waded into it' (lines 9–10) more formally.

12   Why is there a hyphen in the middle of the word 'car-nage' (line 27)?

13   Somewhere between line 30 and the end of the article, there is a play on words. Underline it.

14   There are two reasons why **A car gets the hammer** would not be such an interesting headline. What are they? (Reading the two headlines aloud should help you with one of the reasons.)

15a The first sentence in article A contains the following details.

    a The car had an F-registration.
    b It broke down.
    c The driver had had trouble with it before.
    d It broke down on the M5.

    Find these details in article B.

  b Which style of presentation do you prefer?

> The writers of these two articles have chosen language to make their stories interesting. But they want to make them interesting to different people.

16a The reporter of article B uses 'stormed' (line 6) to describe the way the man moved. It gives the idea of fast movement.

    The words in the box below all describe movement. Decide whether that movement is *fast* or *slow* in each case and write the words in the appropriate column of the table.

amble	rush
bolt	saunter
creep	stalk
dart	~~storm~~
dash	stroll
hare	wander

Fast	*Slow*
storm	creep ✓
dart ✓	hare
dash ✓	saunter ✓
rush ✓	amble ✓
stroll	wander ✓
stalk	bolt

  b The word 'storm' also contains the idea of anger. It describes fast, angry movement.

    What, if anything, do the other words add to the idea of the speed of the movement? (Use a dictionary to help you with this exercise if necessary.)

Reporting the news 2

Section 1 Choice of focus 1

As well as varying their language, reporters may also focus on different aspects of a story, depending on what they think will interest their readers.

1 The two articles below both cover the following facts:

    a Some council workers won a contract.
    b If they had lost it, all 715 of them would have lost their jobs.
    c Because they won it, 236 of them will lose their jobs.

But the directions from which the two reporters approach the story are quite different.

B

Unions save 500 jobs as city
cuts £3m off its rubbish bill

A

Jobs lost as binmen win deal

BINMEN have won a fight to run a city's refuse service . . . . at the cost of 236 jobs.

Council workers beat contractors for refuse deal

By Paul Johnson
Birmingham's refuse men yesterday kept their own jobs when they were awarded the five year contract to empty the city's bins in the face of private sector competition.

    Which of the reporters approaches the story from the positive side?

2 Which of the two articles is more conversational in style? Give an example to support your answer.

3 Article A refers to 'binmen' while article B refers to 'refuse men'. Both articles are talking about the same people, but the phrase used in article A is much more conversational.

    The list on the next page contains pairs of words like this. Complete the table by matching the pairs with the same meaning and then deciding which of the two is more conversational in each case. (Use a dictionary to help you with this exercise if necessary.)

binman
boffin
bus conductress
cabbie
clippie
cop
criminal
crook
policeman
refuse man
scientist
taxi-driver

	Conversational
refuse man	*binman*

4 Look at the headlines below.

C **Sadness for donor mother**

D **Donated embryo implanted in woman**

They come from two different articles on the same story.

One focuses on the human interest aspect of the story. The other is written from the scientific angle. Which is which?

5 Now match the headlines with the beginnings of the articles.

E FOR THE first time a woman has become pregnant with an egg provided by another woman, and fertilised in a laboratory with donated sperm from the hospital's frozen sperm bank.

The woman suffered a spontaneous abortion after 10 weeks.

F A WOMAN pregnant with what would have been the world's first test-tube baby by donor has lost it at ten weeks.

6 Look at the following two articles.

G **THE NAKED body of a pretty girl groom was found yesterday near the site of a Royal horse show.**

Suzanne Thatcher, 18, whose boss is a friend of Prince Philip, had been strangled. She was found in dense undergrowth only 100 yards from the Amberley horse show grounds.

Police said last night that a man had been charged with her murder.

H A 25-year-old man will appear in court at Cirencester, Gloucestershire, today charged with the murder of Miss Suzanne Elizabeth Thatcher, aged 18, whose naked body was found in woodland at Lord Bathurst's 2,000-acre Cirencester Park estate yesterday.

Miss Thatcher, from Bron Manod, Coad Clyw, Blaenauffestiniog, was employed as a groom by a Swansea family who were competing at the Amberley horse show at Cirencester Park.

39

They both cover these points:

a Where the girl was found.
b Who the girl was.
c The fact that a man was arrested for her murder.

But their focus is different

a At first glance, what does it seem each writer considers to be most important?

b Look at the way each writer describes the girl. What details does each article give about her?

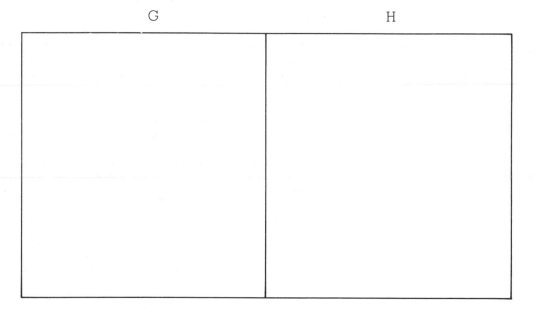

G   H

c What sort of detail does each writer think will interest his/her readers?

d Which article do you prefer and why?

Section 2 Choice of focus 2

This Section looks at the way reporters vary the language and focus of their stories to appeal to the readers they have in mind.

1 The following headlines come from two different articles reporting the same story.

a Which one gives the idea that the baby's life was in great danger?

b Which phrase in particular makes you think this?

2   Now look at the first paragraph of each of the articles.

A A **TINY** baby boy was found abandoned yesterday in a suitcase about to be fed into a dustcart's deadly crusher.

B A **BABY** boy aged three days was in an incubator last night after being found abandoned in a rubbish cupboard at a block of flats.

The table below can be used to compare the focus of the two articles. Tick one box for each article to show what the reader's attention is focused on in each case.

Focus	A	B
a The sex of the baby		
b The potential danger the baby was in		
c The baby's condition now		

3   Which headline gave the more accurate preparation for the story?

4a   Which article gives the less precise description of the baby?

 b   Why did the reporter choose to describe the baby in this way?

5a   The baby was found in a suitcase. Why does article A refer to him as 'Bin babe' and not 'Suitcase babe'?

 b   Why is the headline 'Bin babe . . .' and not 'Bin baby . . .'?

6   Article A refers to a 'tiny baby boy'. The reporter could have written that the baby boy was 'small', but to say that he was 'tiny' is more descriptive.

The words in the box below are more descriptive than the words in the list. Match each word in the box to the word in the list which means the same but is less descriptive. (Use a dictionary for this exercise if necessary.)

more descriptive

boiling
enormous
exhausted
freezing
furious
hilarious
obese
parched
skeletal
soaking
starving
tiny

list	more descriptive
angry	furious ✓
cold	freezing ✓
dry	parched ✓
fat	obese ✓
funny	hilarious ✓
hot	boiling ✓
hungry	starving ✓
large	enormous ✓
small	tiny
thin	skeletal ✓
tired	exhausted ✓
wet	soaking ✓

41

Section 3 Selection of facts

This Section looks at how the focus of articles can be so different that the reporters choose to cover completely different facts.

1   Look at this article on some problems which arose at a nurses' home.

A

> More than 300 nurses on duty over Christmas at Hammersmith Hospital were thawing out yesterday after spending the holiday in freezing unlit rooms.
>
> A power failure plunged the nurses' home at the hospital into darkness on Christmas Day. The girls had to cook by gas stoves and had no heating. Lights and heating were restored yesterday, but there are still no power supplies to the girls' rooms.

a   According to the article, what was the cause of these problems?

b   Write the details the article gives about the nurses' living conditions into the table at the bottom of the page.

2   Here is another article covering the same story

B

> HUNDREDS of nurses were last night shivering with cold in a mice-infested hostel overlooking a jail.
>
> They have already spent their bleakest Christmas ever in freezing, unlit rooms. They had to go to bed to try to keep warm.
>
> A heating and power failure has left them without radios, TV and record players.
>
> Their fridges do not work and food has turned rotten.
>
> 'Bad is too, nice a word for it," said one nurse living in the hostel at London's Hammersmith Hospital.
>
> "The place is a dump. These last few days have been horrible.
>
> "Some girls have been going to bed at eight o'clock to keep warm.
>
> "The trouble is we can't afford to get outside accommodation."
>
> More than 350 girls live at the £43-a-month Hammersmith House. They complain of :—
>
> ● Cramped rooms with not enough space to swing a cat.
> ● Only one kitchen for every 60 girls, with a stove and a fridge.
> ● One bathroom between every 10 nurses.
> ● A plague of mice and sometimes rats.
>
> And nurses on the north side of the building have a room with a view — over Wormwood Scrubs jail.
>
> Another nurse said: "We have permission to sunbathe on the roof in the summer, but who wants to with killers and rapists in the exercise yard below ? "
>
> Now the Royal College of Nursing is to take up the girls' plight.
>
> A spokesman said : " Conditions for nurses living there are bad and something has to be done. We will be acting on their behalf."
>
> The electricity supply failed on Christmas Day as nurses were arranging parties.
>
> Hospital administrator, Mr John Saxby said last night : " It has been a disastrous Christmas. I agree we have problems.
>
> " In the long term we want to provide more kitchens and we have some money to do so.
>
> " One of the troubles is many nurses want to cater for themselves and we just haven't the facilities.
>
> " In the short term we hope to get the heating and power restored in time for New Year's Eve.
>
> " We will be giving a rent refund and paying for food which perished when the fridges shut down."

Complete the table at the bottom of the page with the details of the nurses' living conditions given in article B.

3a   How many of the details in article B are not related to the cause you noted in question 1a.

b   How does the reporter show which details s/he thinks are most important?

Details of the problems at the nurses' home	
A	B

4   Look at the first line of each article.

a When you read 'Hundreds of nurses', how many do you think of?

b Does the phrase 'More than 300 nurses' make you think of more or fewer nurses?

c Instead of starting with 'More than 300 nurses . . .', the writer of article A could have begun like this:

> 'Fewer than 400 nurses . . .'

What difference would this have made?

5   The articles seem to contradict each other on the state of the heating now. Compare the following:

> lines 1–6 (A) and lines 1–5 (B)
> lines 7–15 (A) and lines 75–78 (B)

What is the contradiction?

6   Here are the headlines from the two articles.

C NURSES SHIVERING IN SCANDAL HOSTEL

D NURSES' GLOOMY COLD HOLIDAY

Match the headlines to the articles.

7   The writers expect their stories to get different reactions from their readers.

What reaction does each writer expect? Write the letter of the article beside the appropriate emotion.

	Article
amusement	
indifference	
outrage	
sympathy	

Section 4 Consolidation

This Section looks at the way three different writers report the same story.

1   The extracts below give the opening paragraphs of the three articles.

A FORMER air stewardess and beauty queen who was sacked for allegedly leaving her post "to indulge in horseplay" has settled her claim for unfair dismissal.

Miss Janet Withey, 26, had brought the claim against Air Europe. She was dismissed last January after an incident when her aircraft was refuelling in Portugal.

A Manchester industrial tribunal was told yesterday that terms had been agreed between the parties whereby Miss Withey, of Parsonage Gardens, Handforth, Cheshire, would withdraw her claim on payment of an undisclosed sum.

Earlier she had told the tribunal of her "embarrassment" when cabin steward Mr Andrew Hawrylyszyn had made a joking announcement to the passengers that she had been elected "Miss Lovely Legs Air Europe."

B THE airgirl who "went crackers" on a crowded jet was smiling again yesterday after winning compensation from the airline who sacked her.

5 Ex-beauty queen Janet Withey, fired for crushing cream crackers over a steward's head, withdrew her claim for unfair dismissal after Air Europe offered an out-of-court settlement.

Janet said: "Under the terms of the settlement I am not allowed to tell how much I received — but I am very happy."

10 Earlier an industrial tribunal heard why Janet, 26, gave steward Andrew Hawrylyszyn the cracker treatment.

The ex-Miss Blackpool and Miss UK runner-up said she was annoyed because he pulled her leg about her beauty queen past over the public address system of a holiday jet.

C ANY publicity was good publicity for beauty queen Janet Withey.

5 The former Miss Britain even shaved her head for promotional work.

But after she quit the beauty circuit to become an air hostess, Miss Withey shunned the limelight.

10 And when a colleague reminded passengers of her past, the 26-year-old blonde blew her top.

She showered male steward Andrew Hawrylyszyn with broken cream crackers after he
15 joked about her lovely legs on the aircraft's public address system.

The following outlines show the way the information in the three extracts is organised.

Outline 1

Statement giving background information.
Illustration of this.
More background information.
Details of the incident.

Outline 2

Summary.
Details of settlement.
Details of incident.

Outline 3

Summary.
Details of dismissal.
Details of settlement.
Details of incident.

    a   Match each outline to the appropriate article.

    b   One of the reporters does not start his/her report with a summary. Why do you think s/he chose another starting point?

2   Cross out either *more* or *less* in the table below so that all the statements are correct.

a 'ex-beauty queen' (B, line 4)	is more/less conversational than	'A former . . . beauty queen' (A, line 1)
b '"I am not allowed to tell how much I received"' (B, lines 8–9)	is more/less formal than	'an undisclosed sum' (A, lines 16–17)
c 'Janet, 26,' (B, line 10)	is more/less formal than	'Miss Janet Withey, 26,' (A, line 5)
d 'was annoyed' (B, lines 12–13)	is more/less descriptive than	'blew her top' (C, line 11)
e 'pulled her leg' (B, line 13)	is more/less conversational than	'joked' (C, line 15)

3a   Underline all the words in the three articles which describe or indicate the way Janet Withey felt.

  b   Which article makes most reference to her emotions?

4   Look at article B. What reasons might the reporter have for using 'airgirl' instead of 'air stewardess' in line 1?

5   'Went crackers' (line 1) means the same as 'lost her temper'. What reasons does the reporter have for using the first phrase instead of the second?

6   Look at articles A and B. Which writer creates an intimate, conversational effect in the first paragraph by writing as if the readers already know about Janet Withey?

7   Articles A and B contain the following examples of the use of inverted commas:

    a "went crackers" (B, line 1)
    b "to indulge in horseplay" (A, lines 2–3)
    c "embarrassment" (A, line 19)
    d "Miss Lovely Legs Air Europe" (A, lines 23–24)

As it was pointed out in Unit 2, there are many reasons for putting words in inverted commas. Some of them are listed in the table below.

Decide on the reason for inverted commas in each example and write its letter in the appropriate space in the tables on the next page.

Reasons (unusual use of the language)

Drawing attention to the use of a pun.	
Drawing attention to the use of slang.	
Drawing attention to the use of a technical term.	

Reasons (quotations)

Quoting the title of a book, film, competition etc.	
Quoting a well-known saying.	
Quoting someone else's words.	

8   Now look at articles A and C in full.

A

A FORMER air stewardess and beauty queen who was sacked for allegedly leaving her post "to indulge in horseplay" has settled her claim for unfair dismissal.

Miss Janet Withey, 26, had brought the claim against Air Europe. She was dismissed last January after an incident when her aircraft was refuelling in Portugal.

A Manchester industrial tribunal was told yesterday that terms had been agreed between the parties whereby Miss Withey, of Parsonage Gardens, Handforth, Cheshire, would withdraw her claim on payment of an undisclosed sum.

Earlier she had told the tribunal of her "embarrassment" when cabin steward Mr Andrew Hawrylyszyn had made a joking announcement to the passengers that she had been elected "Miss Lovely Legs Air Europe."

Played jokes

"The passengers all cheered and shouted 'Show us your legs love.' They didn't give me much credit for intelligence — I was just a beauty queen again," she said. Miss Withey admitted retaliating to the joke by sprinkling cream crackers over the steward's head. She said it was common to play jokes on each other in the free time.

Miss Witney added that the incident had happened when the plane was in flight and not on the ground as her employers had claimed. She denied leaving her post unattended and said when she did leave, another stewardess took her place.

Earlier, Mr Desmond de Verteuil, the airline's chief pilot, had told the hearing that Miss Withey had left her post to indulge in some horseplay. "In all my 40 years in civil aviation I have never known such an experience," he said.

Questioned by Mr Stephen Sauvain, counsel for Miss Withey, Mr de Verteuil agreed that he did not interview her before he dismissed her. He as satisfied by statements from witnesses.

C

ANY publicity was good publicity for beauty queen Janet Withey.

The former Miss Britain even shaved her head for promotional work.

But after she quit the beauty circuit to become an air hostess, Miss Withey shunned the limelight.

And when a colleague reminded passengers of her past, the 26-year-old blonde blew her top.

She showered male steward Andrew Hawrylyszyn with broken cream crackers after he joked about her lovely legs on the aircraft's public address system.

However, her bosses didn't see the funny side and sacked 26-year-old Miss Withey for 'gross misconduct'.

Lemonade

Yesterday, after telling her story to an industrial tribunal in Manchester it was announced that an undisclosed settlement had been reached out of court with her former employers, Air Europe.

Miss Withey, of Parsonage Gardens, Handforth, Cheshire, who was claiming unfair dismissal, told the tribunal of other high jinks among cabin staff on the holiday flight — showering water at each other and opening cans of lemonade so they squirted at other staff.

But she said the frolics happened in mid-air and not, as the company claimed, on the ground at Faro in Portugal during a re-fuelling stop between Tenerife and Manchester.

Allegation

And she denied the company's most serious allegation — that she left her post by the rear passenger door breaking safety regulations. Captain Desmond de Verteuil, Air Europe's Operations Director, said that Civil Aviation Authority rules stipulated that front and rear passenger doors had to be manned during refuelling in case of emergency.

He said: 'The CAA would regard her conduct as very serious indeed, to the point where our air operators' certificate could be in jeopardy.

'In more than 40 years I have never come across a similar experience.'

But the captain admitted that he had never interviewed Miss Withey to hear her side of the story.

And the tribunal was told that she was denied the appeal hearing guaranteed to staff in the company's regulations.

Miss Withey said she only learned of the allegations in an interview with the company's Chief of Cabin Staff.

She thought the interview was to be about her application for a more senior post. In fact she was demoted, suspended and later sacked.

The other stewardess on the same flight who sprinkled coffee powder into Mr Hawrylyszyn's crew bag was also sacked.

As she left the court Miss Withey would only say: 'I am delighted with the result.'

The styles of the two articles are different, as you have already seen, but so too is their coverage. Some things are reported in both, some in only one of the articles.

Tick the appropriate boxes in the table below to show where the following details can be found.

	A	C
a Janet Withey's age and address.		
b The name of Janet Withey's legal representative.		
c The plane's destination.		
d Where the hearing took place.		
e The fact that Janet Withey had applied for promotion before she was sacked.		
f The colour of Janet Withey's hair.		
g When Janet Withey was sacked.		
h The fact that Janet Withey claimed the incident happened in mid-air.		
i The fact that another stewardess was also sacked.		
j The fact that members of the crew squirted lemonade at one another as well.		

9   The coverage is different because each article is written to appeal to a different group of readers. Article A is intended for those whose main interest is in the technical details of the dismissal and court case.

What sort of details would you get from article C?

Section 5 Predicting the reader's reaction

This Section looks more closely at the way a reporter makes assumptions about the attitudes and reactions of his/her intended readers.

1   Look at this headline:

Driver in dead trouble

What do you think the article that accompanies it is about?

2   Here is the first paragraph of the article.

> Boston has never been re-nowned as one of America's great centres of law and order — the current Mayor is
> 5 accused of all sorts of skuldug-gery. But the city has now clearly established that, whatever else its citizens may get up to, it is going to accept no
> 10 excuses for illegal parking.

Which of the following means the same as 'skulduggery' (line 5)?

a charitable works
b corrupt behaviour
c devotion to duty

3   The dash at the beginning of line 4 shows that the writer is adding an extra piece of information for the reader. In more formal written English it would not be possible to join the two sentences with a dash.

Which of the following could be used instead of a dash to join the ideas?

a although
b and even
c and furthermore
d but nevertheless

4   What is implied in lines 6–10?

a Boston citizens commit more parking offences than any other kind of offence.
b Penalties for illegal parking in Boston are greater than penalties for any other kind of offence.
c The city authorities are more interested in catching illegal parkers than they are in catching any other kind of offender.

5   Bearing in mind the headline of the article and the paragraph you have just read, what do you expect the next paragraph to be about?

a An example of Boston's tough treatment of parking offenders.
b An example of crime in Boston.
c The activities of Boston's current Mayor.
d None of these.

6   Now read the next paragraph.

> Mr William Hui had put his car in Beacon Street, right in the middle of the city near the public garden. At 10.50 am a
> 15 traffic warden saw it and put a parking ticket on the windscreen. When the car had still not been moved after lunch a second ticket was popped
> 20 under the wiper at 2.30 pm.

Bearing in mind the headline of the article and the paragraph you have just read, what do you expect the next paragraph to be about?

a What else happened to Mr Hui's car.
b What Mr Hui did when he returned.
c Why Mr Hui had not returned.
d None of these.

7   Now look at the next paragraph.

> If none of this seems out of the ordinary, it is worth noting that the car door was wide open and Mr Hui was slumped
> 25 dead over the steering wheel, keys hanging limply in his hand, apparently killed by a gunshot wound in the neck.

What is the double meaning in the headline?

8   Phrases like 'it is worth noting' (line 22) and 'apparently' (line 27) are typical of cautious academic argument.

Bearing in mind the situation, do you think the writer has any need to be cautious in pointing out the facts of the case?

The reporter has deliberately chosen a style of language that is not appropriate to the situation. On several occasions s/he has also prepared the readers to expect something and then has presented them with something else.

The creation of a gap between what is expected, on the one hand, and what actually happens or exists, on the other, is called *irony*.

Its effect is intended to be humorous.

9 Here are the final paragraphs of the article.

> After he had lain there for
> 30 something like 6½ hours col-
> lecting posthumous parking
> tickets, a passerby, as it is offi-
> cially recorded, "became suspi-
> cious and called the police."
> 35 The police department's
> spokesman said later, with pro-
> per Boston restraint, that
> it was "not clear" why the traf-
> fic warden — known as meter
> 40 maids in America — had not
> also become suspicious, or, at
> least, tried to tackle Mr Hui
> about his parking habits —
> 45 given that he was hanging
> around at the time.
>   "The homicide unit will
> have to find out who the meter
> maid was and talk to her," he
> said.
> 50 It was not clear last night
> what would happen about the
> parking tickets.

a Why is it a contradiction of talk of anyone collecting anything posthumously?

b What effect does the reporter achieve by using this contradiction in lines 30–31?

10a What is usually awarded posthumously?

b What effect is created by the combination of 'posthumous parking tickets' in line 31?

11 Which of the following is the main source of irony in lines 29–34?

　　a The fact that the passerby's suspicions were written down in official records.
　　b The fact that it was 6½ hours before anyone called the police to the dead man.
　　c The fact that the passerby called the police instead of calling the traffic warden.

12 The reporter continues to use this ironical style to the end of the article.

a In using irony throughout the artical, the reporter assumes that the readers will share his/her own reaction to the incident.

What is that reaction?

　　a Amazement—that a dead man in the middle of a city should be ignored for so long.
　　b Horror—that a man could be brutally shot in the middle of a city.
　　c Admiration—that the Boston City police are so methodical.

b What effect would this article have if the reader didn't share the reporter's attitude?

For irony to be effective, the reader and the reporter must share the same attitude to the subject.

UNIT 4
Comment

Section 1 Background to the news

This Section deals with an article which gives background details to a news story and at the same time comments on the news.

1 Read very quickly through the article below and decide which of the following it is about. (Don't take more than one minute.)

a Legal history   c Public transport
b Motoring   d The police

NO one should think that, because the train strike is on, they are free of all parking restrictions.

5   In London, emergency parking facilities are being provided in some of the Royal parks. But that is all. Normal restrictions apply to parking on yellow lines and at meters—and
10 all the other parking laws still endure.

Target

The law is clear, and has been for at least 160 years. In 1812, before German engineer Karl Benz inven-
15 ted the motor car, Lord Ellenborough, then Lord Chief Justice, ruled : 'Every unauthorised obstruction on the highway to the annoyance of the King's subjects is an
20 indictable offence . . . no one can make a stable-yard of the King's highway.'
Our only legal right is to use the highway 'for passing and re-
25 passing', as a judge at the turn of the century put it.

And that is the basis that could lead any motorist today to believe that he is an easy target for a
30 traffic warden or policeman anxious to notch up another conviction. There is no section of the community more set upon, more beset by the authorities, more likely to
35 end up in trouble with the law than drivers.

Just look at these cases :
● a 34-year-old holidaymaker in Brixham, Devon, parks in a quiet
40 side street. He checks there are no yellow lines but comes back to find a parking ticket stuck to his windscreen—and still-wet yellow lines painted on either side of, and
45 underneath, his car. Workmen, repainting the surface of the road, had pushed his car to and fro to replace the lines.

● A housewife parks in a muni-
50 cipal car park in a small Buckinghamshire town. She puts her money in a meter that should have given her a ticket. But it is out of order. So what happens ? She is summoned
55 —and convicted—for failing to display the ticket she had paid for but not received.
● Two council workmen painting double yellow lines along a road in
60 Newton Abbot, Devon, are amazed to see a traffic warden putting a parking ticket on their van. Comments the County Surveyor : 'The traffic warden was doing his job.'

Waiting

65   ● A solicitor parks in a meter zone outside his Mayfair flat to fetch his elderly wife. He has only one lung and cannot move quickly. He has to wait for a lift to come
70 down and it is five minutes before he is back at the car with his wife.
'Persons to be picked up means persons who are ready and waiting

to be picked up, not persons who
75 might be ready inside ten or 20 minutes,' says the magistrate, who convicts him.
And as if all this were not enough, motorists have a new 'goodie' lying
80 in wait for them. We are soon going to have in London—for an experimental period only, we are assured —a frightening device called a wheel clamp.
85   The police put it on one or more wheels of your car and you cannot then move the vehicle until you phone the nearest police station and ask them to remove it—which they
90 will when you pay an instant fine !
'A totally un-British idea and likely to worsen police-public relations,' said a Tory back-bencher in a Commons debate this year when
95 MPs agreed to give the Metropolitan Police power to try out this experiment.
So what else is new ? It's like the true story of the man who asked
100 his local council to paint double yellow lines outside his house to prevent others blocking his drive and then found that he was the first to receive a ticket.
105   Fellow motorists, we simply cannot win !

A 'back-bencher' is a Member of Parliament who doesn't hold a position of responsibility in the Government or Opposition.

2 Read the first two paragraphs more carefully (lines 1–11). Which of the following does the writer mean?

a It is unreasonable to expect parking restrictions to be relaxed because of the train strike.
b It is a mistake to expect parking restrictions to be relaxed because of the train strike.
c It is unlikely that anyone would expect parking restrictions to be relaxed because of the train strike.

3 In lines 17–22, the writer quotes a ruling by a former Lord Chief Justice. What were the 'obstructions' he referred to most likely to be?

    a animals
    b cars
    c people

4 What does 'that' (2nd word, line 27) refer to?

5 According to lines 27–36, the motorist may feel that he is an easy target for a certain kind of traffic warden or policeman. What kind?

    a ambitious
    b conscientious
    c frightened

6 What is the writer's main point?

    a Motorists often break the law.
    b Motorists are often victimised by the authorities.
    c The authorities are usually sympathetic to motorists.

7 The writer quotes four cases. How does s/he draw the reader's attention to them?

8 Match the halves of the sentences below to make statements about the four cases.

1 A Buckinghamshire housewife put money in the ticket machine . . .	*a* . . . while the car was parked there.
2 The Mayfair solicitor was fined . . .	*b* . . . there were no yellow lines on the road.
3 Two council workmen in Devon were fined . . .	*c* . . . although the machine had been faulty.
4 When the Brixham holidaymaker parked his car . . .	*d* . . . because he was parked illegally for five minutes.
5 The court convicted her for failing to have a ticket . . .	*e* . . . but got no ticket.
6 Yellow lines were painted on the road . . .	*f* . . . for parking on the double yellow lines which they were painting.

9 The writer's argument consists of two parts: his/her main point followed by the four cases mentioned above.

Which of the alternatives below shows the correct relationship between the two parts?

MAIN POINT

    a 4 less important points giving the same side of the argument.

    b 4 examples to illustrate and support the main point.

    c 4 related points that give the other side of the argument.

10 Which of the following statements is true?

    a The writer says that these cases are typical.
    b The writer says that these cases are unusual.
    c The writer doesn't say whether the cases are typical or unusual.

11 Underline the phrase which the writer then uses to show that s/he is going to introduce more evidence of the same kind.

12 The word "goodie" (line 79) is in inverted commas to draw attention to the fact that there is something unusual about the language the writer is using. What, in particular, is the writer drawing attention to?

    a The use of irony.
    b The writer's use of a nickname or his own term for something.
    c The use of a pun.
    d The use of slang.
    e The use of a technical term in non-technical writing.

13 What does 'which' (line 89) refer to?

14 A Tory back-bench MP describes the wheel clamp as 'totally un-British' (line 91). Which of the following does s/he mean?

    a The wheel clamp will be imported.
    b The idea of introducing wheel clamps has come from abroad.
    c The idea of fitting wheel clamps is contrary to British ways.

15 Which of the following would make the best headline for the article?

    a **Drivers no longer kings of the road . . .**

    b **Making the law-breakers toe the yellow line**

    c **No escape from the perils of parking**

    d **Police to 'clamp down' on London motorists!**

16 Do you find the argument well-balanced and convincing?

Opinion writers can make their comment through:

a carefully selecting their facts.
b their choice of language.

News articles also vary both these features which makes it hard sometimes to tell where reporting ends and comment begins.

Section 2 A regular comment column

This Section looks at one day's contribution from a humorous columnist, in his regular feature called 'Moreover . . .' (See page 52.)

Look at the first part of this article (extract A) and then answer questions 1 and 2.

  1 Do you think the claims made for the Diet (lines 10–12) and dietary fibre (lines 15–19) are reasonable?

  2a Write the word you think is missing from line 5: _____

    b Write in the most likely endings to these two sentences.

     'Yes, one day is all you need to reach slimming perfection, life-long dietary

     control and _____
     (lines 12–13)

'From it comes promotion at work, a successful marriage and _____

_____' (lines 19–20)

A

> Fibre!
>   That's the name of the slimming game.
>   Last year it was grapefruit.
> 5 Next year it will be _____.
>   But this year fibre is where it's all at. And this column is, as usual, up with the trendsetters.
>   Start today, with the Moreover One-
> 10 Day Fibre Diet! Yes, one day is all you need to reach slimming perfection, life-long dietary control and _____
>
>   Fibre, we now know, unlocks the
> 15 secret path to perfect fitness. It gives you charisma and that inner glow which lets you know that your bowels are a credit. From it comes promotion at work, a successful marriage and _____
> 20 _____

3a The word missing from line 5 is 'sand'.

Is this the kind of answer you expected?

b The sentences finish like this:

'. . . a deep red complexion.' (lines 12–13)
'. . . much less washing up.' (lines 19–20)

Are these claims in keeping with the exaggerated ones made in the earlier parts of the sentences?

c What effect does the writer hope to create by choosing these endings?

4 Here is the next part of the article.

B

> That's because fibre is all *natural*. It's organic material which has been untouched by manufacturing, advertising, or mentions in newspaper diary features.
> 25 It's simple, delicious, brown and chewy. Sugar isn't. It's also good for keeping out draughts. Sugar isn't either.
>   A life-long fibre diet could be boring if you're not used to it. That's why
> 30 we've devised this One-Day Fibre Crash Course. Just follow it and we guarantee you'll feel totally different.
>
>   Day One (*unlike most diets, this is also the last day*).

a The 'Moreover. . .' column appears regularly in the *Times* newspaper. It could be described as a diary feature. Bearing this in mind, how would you describe line 24?

b What effect is this supposed to have?

5 In lines 25–27, the writer mentions that fibre possesses an unusual quality for a food. Underline this quality.

6 How could lines 31–32 be ambiguous?

7 What do you expect to follow lines 33–34?

    a details of a humorous diet.
    b details of a serious diet.

8 Here is the next part of the article. As you can see, each box contains two different ways of completing the article.

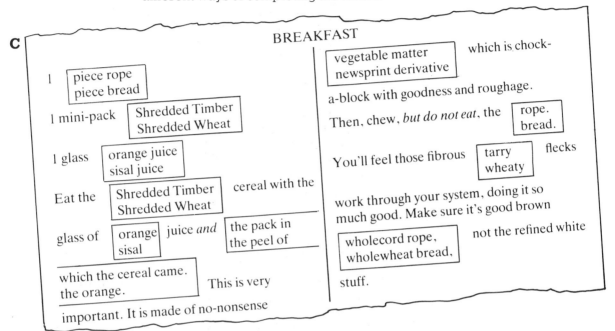

Cross out one of the choices in each box to complete the article in the appropriate style.

9 Here is the rest of the article.

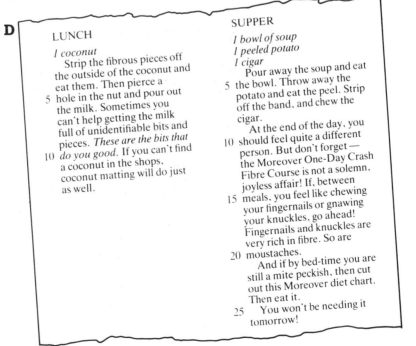

How would you describe the writer's suggestion for a high-fibre lunch?

10 Is there any ambiguity about feeling 'different' in line 10 under 'Supper'?

11a Underline the part of extract D that tells you that the Diet can be fun.

 b What 'fun' is the dieter allowed?

 c When might you normally feel the need to do these things?

12 If you followed the Diet, would you expect to be 'a mite peckish' (D, 'Supper', line 22) by bed-time?

13a What is the writer's attitude to health food and dieting?

 b How does he make his point?

  a By careful argument.
  b By firmly stating his position over and over.
  c By selecting only the facts that support his position.
  d By the use of irony.

 c Do you find this kind of argument effective?

> The use of irony reveals something about the attitude of the writer. When it is in an extreme form—as it is in this article—it is an indirect way of making a very strong comment.

Section 3 A television review

1 Look at the first two paragraphs of this review of a television programme.

A

> SPEAKING over the dead body of Julius Caesar, Mark Antony, in Shakespeare's play, says: "If you have tears, prepare to shed them now."
>
> 5 If you have tears, prepare to shed them tonight at 9.30, when BBC2 screens a programme called "Rabbits Don't Cry."

Do they appeal to your logic or your emotions?

2 The rest of the article is opposite.

a Underline the writer's definition of vivisection.

b Here is an objective definition from a dictionary:

Vivisection—dissection or other painful treatment of living animals for purposes of scientific research.

Circle the words in the writer's definition that show his/her attitude to vivisection.

3 Look at lines 24–30. Circle the phrase which shows that the writer is not reporting his/her own opinion in these lines.

4 Which of the following diagrams gives the best illustration of the relationship between *animal experiments* and *vivisection*?

a animal experiments = vivisection   *b* animal experiments
                    vivisection

c vivisection
  animal experiments

"Rabbits Don't Cry" is about vivisection—the persevering and systematic cruelty to, and mutilation of, animals in laboratories up and down the United Kingdom in the supposed interests of improved medical care for human beings, safer cosmetics for women and improved scientific knowledge.

The reason for the programme's evocative title is simple :—

Rabbits have no tear ducts, and cannot cry. This makes them, in the judgement of the scientists, particularly suited for the testing of new shampoos and bleaches.

In the interests of making it easier and safer for human beings to wash their hair, thousands of rabbits are tortured to blindness every year.

That is only the very tip of the iceberg. About half a million experiments are carried out in Britain each year, many involving large numbers of animals.

One animal somewhere dies *every six seconds* as a result of vivisection. And more than *80 per cent* of the experiments are carried out without anaesthetics.

Yet there has only been **ONE** successful prosecution for cruelty under the relevant Act in over 100 years.

In his novel " The Plague Dogs "—the most powerful anti-vivisectionist tract I have ever read—Richard Adams, author of " Watership Down," details experiments being carried out on pigeons to discover the origins and nature of their homing instinct.

Some are blinded. Others are fitted with contact lenses. Others have their feet, beaks, nostrils, mouths or lungs impaired. Still others are confined, before testing flights, in cages where there is perpetual rain, or perpetual sunshine.

" The result of all these experiments so far." Adams writes with chilling and sarcastic restraint, " had been most informative, yielding the basic information that while some of the birds succeeded in returning home, others did **not.**"

I confess to being something of an extremist on this subject. I would, for example, if I had the power, ban forthwith all vivisection, whatever its declared purpose, medical or other.

Richard Adams, when I spoke to him earlier this week, was surprised to find somebody who took an even harder line than he did.

But he said : " If I could be convinced that any particular experiment on an animal served a direct medical purpose— if there was a straight line between the experiment and the cure—then I would find it justifiable.

" What is horrible is the thought of the many thousands of experiments undertaken simply to serve scientific curiosity or, worse, to pamper human beings."

Adams proposes a Royal Commission to investigate what is going on.

What has so far protected the vivisectionists from the righteous anger of a nation is, first, the blanket of secrecy that covers their work and, second, the vague general conviction that experiments lead directly to improvements in treating human illness.

It must be said as loudly and clearly and as often as possible that this is just not true.

For one thing, a great many experiments are carried out—like those on the pigeons — solely to satisfy (or not, as the case may be) the curiosity of the experimenters.

For another, the majority of remaining cases are concerned with the testing of cosmetics — lipsticks, **face** powders, whatever.

Think on it for a moment : Is it really worth it ?

The other day I came home to find a large dog lying outside my door. He was in a bad shape, bleeding and bruised.

I gave the police a description of him and took him to my vet. The vet told me that, apart from being hit by a car the dog had been half-starved and systematically beaten with a stick.

Yet what that dog—I have since adopted it— suffered in the past bears no resemblance whatsoever to what many thousands of dogs, cats, mice, rats, hamsters, birds suffer every day, and are suffering as you read this piece.

That dog's owner could be fined, forbidden to keep another domestic animal ; even imprisoned.

The scientists go their merry and sadistic way in peace, secure in the knowledge that anxious humanity outside the walls of their laboratories believe — however naively — that they are doing a good job for people.

The Commission's terms of reference, he says, should be based " on the assumption that the use of animals in medical and scientific investigation should be reduced to the lowest possible number."

---

5 According to the writer's argument in lines 37–49, which of the following is true?

   a 80% of animal experiments are performed without anaesthetic.
   b 80% of vivisection experiments are performed without anaesthetic.

6 Here is a more detailed report of this part of the TV programme, from another reviewer.

B

Rabbits Don't Cry was indeed a partisan cry of rage, directed not only against lab. researchers, but also against the new breed of factory farming which condemns pigs, cows and poultry to entire lifetimes spent in dank, foul-smelling cages never penetrated by fresh air or sunshine.

'Conditions,' said Richard Ryder, a former Chairman of the RSPCA, 'are worse than some of the concentration camps in the war.' The vast number of animal experiments, he added, were useless to mankind; eight out of ten were performed without anaesthetic.

According to this report of what was said, which of the alternatives in question 5 is true?

7 The writer of article A says that there has been 'only ONE successful prosecution . . . under the relevant Act' (lines 50–54). This suggests that there have been other unsuccessful attempts to prosecute under this Law.

There could be two possible reasons for the lack of success:

   a The Act is not being enforced properly.
   b The experiments haven't broken the Law.

Circle the word in that paragraph which tells you that the writer thinks the first reason is responsible.

8 Look at lines 65–82 of article A. The writer uses an experiment on pigeons as evidence in his/her argument.

a What is the source of this evidence?

b Is it usual to use this kind of source to build up a factual argument?

9 According to Richard Adams (lines 74–82), which of the following is true of the experiment with pigeons?

> a It gave no new information about the origins or the nature of the homing instinct in birds.
> b It gave some information about the nature of the homing instinct in birds.
> c It gave some information about the nature of the homing instinct in blind pigeons.

10a What does the word 'what' (line 106) refer to?

b What do lines 106–112 tell you about Richard Adams' attitude to scientific curiosity?

11 According to lines 116–126, which of the following is true of the British public?

> a They approve of what is going on in experimental laboratories.
> b They are outraged by what is going on in experimental laboratories.
> c The don't know what is going on in experimental laboratories.

12 Look at lines 146–180 where the writer makes a comparison.

a Are the following statements true or false, according to the writer's argument in these lines?

a Scientists are like dog owners.	true	false
b The dog owner had been deliberately cruel.	true	false
c The dog hadn't suffered much.	true	false
d Many laboratory animals suffer more than the dog did.	true	false
e Scientists are unlikely to be penalised for the ill-treatment of animals.	true	false
f Scientists are happy people.	true	false
g Scientists enjoy making animals suffer.	true	false
h It is naïve of scientists to feel secure.	true	false

b Do you think the comparison made in these lines is a good one?

13 Which of the following sentences would be the best ending for article A?

> a Surely this is something we should ultimately be aiming for.
>
> c Surely this is the very least we should insist upon.
>
> b Surely this is taking the whole thing a bit too far.
>
> d Surely this is not enough for the following very good reasons.

14 Does the writer argue convincingly?

Do you agree or disagree with his/her attitude to vivisection and animal experiments?

> Writers may try to make their arguments convincing by appealing to the emotions of their readers rather than logic.

Section 4 Editorial comment 1

This Section looks at two Editorials (one from *The Daily Mail* and one from *The Sun*) commenting on the progress of a Private Member's Bill—that is, a Bill put before Parliament by a back-bench MP—to change the law on the hours that shops can open.

A

THE battle is on to allow shops to open on Sunday if they choose. An MP is bringing in a Private Member's Bill. And this one will have Government backing.

But let nobody underestimate the spoiling tactics of those still lobbying to nobble this popular measure. If the unions, the Sabbatarians, yes, and some retail groups can keep the legal shutters up, they will.

The Daily Mail has long crusaded for greater shopping freedom. We shall not relax now in our determination to see that you are really being served by the Parliament you elected.

B

HOPES of a revolution in our antiquated shopping laws have received a setback.

The Government has said it won't help a back bench MP get his Bill to allow late hour and Sunday shopping through the Commons.

That's a pity.

As The Sun pointed out earlier this year, the present Sunday trading laws are ludicrous. Many town halls don't bother to enforce them.

Ministers should ignore the Sunday killjoy lobby and help sweep the reform through.

Then they can turn their attention to our crazy licensing laws.

1 Do the articles express the same view about the shopping laws?

2 What has changed in the situation between the printing of article A and article B?

3 Look at article A. Underline the phrase later in the article which means the opposite of 'to allow shops to open' (line 1).

4a To 'lobby' (line 7) means to try to get support for something. What does 'this popular measure' (line 8) refer to?

b Who are 'those still lobbying to nobble this popular measure' (lines 7–8)?

5 Which of the following do you think means the same as 'to nobble' (line 8)?

   a to make it easier for something to happen.
   b to stop something from happening.

   Now check in a dictionary for the exact meaning of 'nobble'.

6 What does the use of phrases like 'spoiling tactics' (lines 6–7) and 'to nobble' (line 8) show about the writer's attitude?

7 Look at line 9. Putting 'yes' into the middle of a sentence can mean one of two things:

   a The writer anticipates that the reader will be surprised by what follows.
   b The writer anticipates that the reader will be expecting what follows.

   Which of the two possibilities is the case here?

8 The writer of article A borrows language more normally used in the context of war to describe the situation. List the words and phrases s/he uses.

9   Look at article B.

a   What source does the writer quote to support his/her claim that the laws are ridiculous?

b   Does this, in your opinion, support his/her case well?

10   Lines 10–12 contain two ideas:

The present trading laws are ludicrous.
Many town halls don't bother to enforce them.

One of the following alternatives could be used to join the ideas into one sentence. Write it in the sentence below.

a although
b and so
c because

The present trading laws are ludicrous_____ many town halls don't bother to enforce them.

11a   The writer of article A mentions the 'unions, the Sabbatarians, yes, and some retail groups' in lines 9–10.

How does the writer of article B refer to the same group of people?

b   Which part of this phrase shows the attitude of the writer of article B?

12   Match each of these headlines to the appropriate article, explaining the double meaning in each case.

C

D

13   What makes the style of argument in article A more formal?

14a   Do the articles give the cases for *and* against the change in the law?

b   Which article do you prefer?

> Opinion writers sometimes attempt to make their case by stating one side of the argument very assertively. The points are usually made briefly—sometimes in one-sentence paragraphs—and are often emphasised by the use of visual techniques, such as underlining. Generally speaking they appeal to the readers' emotions rather than logical reasoning.

Section 5 Editorial comment 2

This Section looks at another Editorial.

1   The eight paragraphs of the article opposite have been numbered. From the nine headings below, choose the one that best describes the contents of each paragraph. Write its number in the space provided in each case.

Heading	Paragraph no.
a The official reaction to the inhabitants' proposals.	
b The current attitude to the treatment of the handicapped.	
c Suggestions for Teignmouth in the future.	
d The gap between theory and reality.	

e The behaviour of some so-called 'normal' people.	
f Attempts to return to previous values.	
g The grounds for the inhabitants' displeasure.	
h Where Teignmouth's attitude might lead.	
i The light in which the town has appeared.	

Teignmouth's gritted teeth

1 Every so often, ministers and civil servants who may be trying to produce decent, humane and enlightened policies must be brought up short by a glimpse of the chasm
5 that exists between themselves and the public, between policy and practice. The people of Teignmouth have this week afforded us just such a glimpse in the row over holidays for the mentally handicapped.

2 10 Townsfolk and local traders have been protesting that mentally handicapped holiday-makers are driving out other tourists. At the centre of the argument is a hotel which caters particularly for mentally ill
15 and handicapped people. Local people have been complaining that they have been driving away trade by such anti-social actions as vomiting in pubs or urinating in the street. Children have been approached on the beach
20 by these people and have run away screaming as a result. Helpful suggestions have included restricting the number of handicapped holiday-makers and herding them all into a hotel on the edge of Dartmoor.

3 25 It was suggestions like these which prompted Mr Brian Rix, the secretary-general of Mencap, to accuse the locals of promoting a kind of apartheid for the handicapped. And the level of prejudice and ignorance behind
30 the protest is startling. During the whole of last year, only some 22 per cent of the residents of the hotel in question were mentally handicapped.

4 It is not clear whether they are objecting to
35 the mentally handicapped in particular, or to all handicapped people in general. What is clear is that they have succeeded in depicting Teignmouth quite unjustifiably as some kind of sequel to The Midwich Cuckoos*, a
40 strange and frightening place where the people are odd.

5 Not only are these fears absurdly exaggerated, they quite irrationally single out the handicapped for blame. People who
45 suffer from no handicap at all are occasionally sick in pubs. Some of them have even been known to urinate in the streets. Young, able-bodied men and women have been known to do far worse in holiday resorts. Yet
50 no one would consider imposing a quota for young people as a result, or herding them into a hotel on the edge of Dartmoor.

6 We now, quite rightly, encourage integration for the handicapped. Locking people
55 away behind high walls, away from the able-bodied, is now seen to be unjust and immensely damaging. It is considered their right to enjoy holidays by the sea, not hidden away from view but as part of the wider society in
60 which they have a place.

7 This requires a degree of tolerance which the able-bodied once had but now appear, sadly, to have lost. Once, village idiots were accepted by the community. As society be-
65 came industrialised, it started to lock them away. Now, we are trying to restore the earlier tolerance. As Mr Rix commented, hundreds of modern resorts accommodate the handicapped with no complaint.

8 70 If the people of Teignmouth had their way, we would indeed be on a slippery slope. It seems a dotty, sick way to run a holiday town.

---

* *The Midwich Cuckoos* is the title of a science-fiction novel by John Wyndham, in which the inhabitants of a town called Midwich are taken over by non-humans from outer space.

2 Mark the statement which is true according to lines 1–3.

a Ministers and civil servants are allowed to try and produce decent, humane and enlightened policies.
b Ministers and civil servants are probably trying to produce decent, humane and enlightened policies.
c Ministers and civil servants are unlikely to be trying to produce decent, humane and enlightened policies.

3a What is likely to bring someone 'up short' (line 4)?

a Something boring.
b Something satisfying.
c Something surprising.

b Which of these phrases could replace 'must be' in line 3?

a . . . are probably . . .
b . . . feel the need to be . . .
c . . . ought to be . . .

4a What does 'such' (line 8) refer to?

 b Who does 'these people' (line 20) refer to?

 c Who does 'the locals' (line 27) refer to?

5 Underline the word that shows the writer doesn't really think the 'suggestions' mentioned in line 21 are 'helpful'.

6 Find the evidence the writer uses to support the two claims below and write the line numbers in the table.

Claims	Evidence
a The inhabitants' fears are absurdly exaggerated.	lines _____
b It is irrational to single out the handicapped for blame.	lines _____

7a In lines 44–45, the reporter writes about 'people who suffer from no handicap at all'. How does s/he refer to the same people again in paragraph 7?

 b In line 50, the reporter writes of imposing a quota. How did s/he refer to the same thing in paragraph 2?

8 On several occasions in the article, the writer openly comments on a statement.

Look at the statements in the table below and decide whether the writer agrees or disagrees with each one. If you think s/he agrees with the statement, put a tick (✓) in the box beside it. If you think s/he disagrees with the statement, put a cross (✗) in the box beside it. In the final column of the table, write the word or words which gave you the answer in each case.

Statements	✓/✗	Words
a Teignmouth is like a sequel to the fictional town of Midwich.		
b Handicapped people should be integrated into society.		
c It is unfortunate that the able-bodied are intolerant.		

9 What do you think is meant by being 'on a slippery slope' (line 71)?

  a ... that things are likely to get better.
  b ... that things are likely to get worse.

10 Here are four phrases which have been deleted from the article. Show in each case where the phrase has come from by writing its letter in the appropriate place in the article.

  a ... – and in many areas it is working.
  b ... – hardly a proportion to flood the town.
  c ... – like wrecking them.
  d ... – quotas for the handicapped today, restrictions for the elderly tomorrow.

11a Do you think the writer argues his/her case convincingly?

  b Do you agree with his/her point of view?

> An opinion writer can make his/her case by presenting both sides of the argument and then defending the ones s/he agrees with. This kind of reasoned argument involves producing evidence to back up points and linking ideas logically.
> Its main appeal is to logic and reason rather than to the emotions of the reader.

UNIT 5
Reporting sport

Section 1 Making reporting economical

You have already noticed in Unit 2, Sections 1 and 3, how reporters save space by piling information before and after a noun. This feature plays a particularly important part in sports reporting.

Look at this example:

FOOTBALL

BOTTOM-of-the-table Birmingham put up a tremendous fight against run away leaders Liverpool at Anfield.

In standard written English, the information would probably appear in a phrase or clause:

Birmingham, at the bottom of the table, put up a . . .
or Birmingham, who are bottom of the table, put up a . . .

But for the sake of economy, the reporter has taken the most important words from the clause, put them in front of the noun and coined an adjective:

Bottom-of-the-table Birmingham put up a . . .

1 The extracts below contain examples of information which has been expressed in this economical way. Find the examples and then rewrite them so that they would be acceptable in standard English.

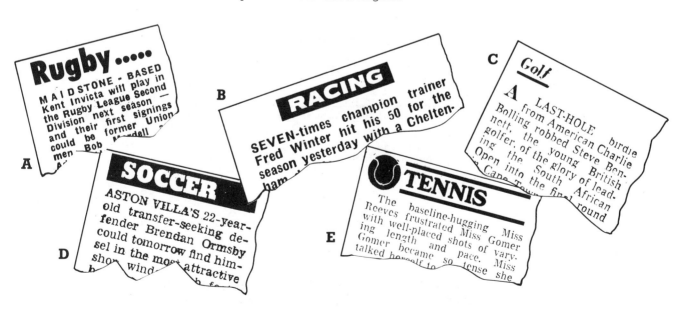

A Rugby .....
MAIDSTONE - BASED Kent Invicta will play in the Rugby League Second Division next season — and their first signings could be former Union men Bob Mandell

B RACING
SEVEN-times champion trainer Fred Winter hit his 50 for the season yesterday with a Cheltenham

C Golf
A LAST-HOLE birdie from American Charlie Bolling robbed Steve Bennett, the young British golfer, of the glory of leading the South African Open into the final round at Cape Town

D SOCCER
ASTON VILLA'S 22-year-old transfer-seeking defender Brendan Ormsby could tomorrow find himself in the most attractive show window

E TENNIS
The baseline-hugging Miss Reeves frustrated Miss Gomer with well-placed shots of varying length and pace. Miss Gomer became so tense she talked herself

2 The next extract is longer. Rewrite the description of the jockey—you will probably have to make several sentences. You will also need to refer to the rest of the article.

61

> Hangovers have always affected different jockeys in different ways and a New Year's Eve party which lasted well into 1983 was clearly no handicap whatever to George Sloan at Newbury yesterday.
>
> It never looked like hindering the 42-year-old ex-champion amateur Tennessee-based health spa impressario and Transatlantic commuter as he rode his wife's Earthstopper to victory in the Bradstone Mandarin Handicap Chase.

When sports reporters use clauses following a noun, they very often include far more information than would be acceptable for a clause in standard English.

Look at the example:

The clause beginning 'who won . . .' contains the following information:

SNOOKER

Steve Davis, <u>who won the £16,000 first prize in the Lada Classic by taking the last four frames to beat Bill Werbeniuk 9-5,</u> will precede his defence of the Benson and Hedges Masters title by playing exhibitions in Dubai and Bahrain this week with Terry Griffiths, who last year beat him 9-8 on the final black in the Lada final.

a Steve Davis won the first prize.
b It was in the Lada Classic.
c It was worth £16,000.
d He took the last four frames.
e He beat Werbeniuk.
f The score was 9–5.

In standard English, this information could be expressed in many ways, for example:

Steve Davis won the first prize, worth £16,000, in the Lada Classic. He took the last four frames to beat Bill Werbeniuk by 9–5.

or

Steve Davis beat Bill Werbeniuk in the Lada Classic. He took the £16,000 prize with a score of 9–5 after winning the last four frames.

3 Here are some more extracts from sports reports.

Break down the information in each of the underlined clauses. Then put the information together again in a form which would be acceptable in standard English.

Hockey   **A**

SOUTHPORT, <u>who toppled Walton, the then leaders, last weekend to take over at the top of the Northern Premier Indoor League table on goal difference,</u> themselves face a demanding test in their four-match programme at the Richard Dunn Sports Centre, Bradford, this afternoon

a _____

b _____

c _____

d _____

e _____

_____

_____

_____

B

GOLF

Cherry, who defies all golf theory by driving majestically and putting devastatingly with a left arm that is permanently b e n t following an operation eight weeks ago, picked up his biggest pay-out —the £3,000 first prize.

a
b
c
d
e
f

C

Lawn Tennis

Jose Higueras, the Spanish No. 1, ranked eighth in the world who outplayed reigning World champion Jimmy Connors, to reach the semi-finals of the French Championships last year, is top-seeded to win this £16,000 British Hard Court Championship title.

a
b
c
d
e
f

D

Horse~racing

DAVID ELSWORTH, who has enjoyed his best-ever season under National Hunt rules and was at Newbury saddling Vivaque to finish second to Ash King in the Tote Credit Hurdle, landed the Willim Hill Lincoln Handicap with Mighty Fly at Doncaster **writes Richard Baerlein.**

a
b
c
d
e
f
g

Section 2 Making reporting clear

Like any other reporter, the sports reporter is concerned as much with clarity as economy.

1 The paragraphs in the middle section of the football report below are in the wrong order. Using the kind of reference clues already discussed in Unit 2, complete the table to show the correct order of the paragraphs.

A

Wrong picture

Stoke 1, Ipswich 0

STOKE manager Ritchie Barker was voicing his belief before the game with Ipswich that the future of football depended perhaps on boys playing for their local clubs, writes **William Keenan.**

B Against Ipswich he brought in 18-year-old former apprentice Ian Painter who proved the point by winning the goal for Stoke. Young Painter's goal in the 57th minute, a header from the left wing corner, broke the deadlock and also helped to atone for Stoke's earlier misses.

C It would also, he argued, bring back a greater community feeling between teams and their local public.

D And from another corner O'Callaghan once again obliged with a back header which dropped at the feet of Berry, once again standing on the goal line. But the Stoke defender tried to kick the ball through Ipswich's prostrate keeper rather than overhead and the ball was cleared.

F With his appalling injury situation he had both the opportunity and the necessity to put his theory into practice.

E They went straight into attack from the kick off and won a corner on the right. O'Callaghan's back header from the kick went straight on to the head of central defender Berry who was virtually standing on the goal line. But Berry's header hit the crossbar.

G In one of the most hard-fought and exciting games seen at Stoke this season the home side did about 90 per cent of the attacking in the first half and should have taken the lead after just 80 seconds.

H After the Stoke goal Ipswich played with more determination and pushed more players into the Stoke penalty area. Thijssen headed just over and then Gates raised the ball high and wide

1 A	2	3	4	5	6	7	8 H

Section 3 Preparing the reader for the article

To help clarify their writing reporters often provide summaries of what they are about to write. This prepares the reader for the way the information has been organised.

1 Look at the first paragraph of this report on a horse race.

A

LESLEY ANN BACK TO FORM

LESLEY ANN led the way in shattering two pre-conceived ideas when she won the Anthony Mildmay,
5 Peter C a z a l e t Memorial Handicap 'Chase at Sandown Park on Saturday.

How is the information that follows this first paragraph likely to be organised?

a | first: details of Lesley Ann's past performance.
    then: details of the two preconceived ideas.

b | first: history of the Anthony Mildmay, Peter Cazalet Memorial Handicap Chase.
    then: details of the two preconceived ideas.

c | first: details of the two preconceived ideas.
    then: discussion of why they were shattered.

2 Now look at the rest of the article.

'odds-on' is a betting term, the odds given when a horse is strong favourite to win a race. The winnings would amount to less than the original stake.

As one of four runners who rose within two lengths of each
10 other at the third-last fence, she played her part in a thrilling finish to a race whose five-horse turn-out had threatened anti-climax.
15 And in outstaying odds-on Fifty Dollars More on the climb from the final fence to win by two-and-a-half lengths, she flattened the theory that the favourite's close
20 second in the King George VI 'Chase at Kempton Park, made him a certainty on his return to handicap company.

Whether Kempton took its toll
25 and Fifty Dollars More ran below his best here, or whether the Kempton feature was a misleading race in the first place, cannot be said with certainty.
30 There is though, no doubting Lesley Ann's return to peak form after starting the season with a well-beaten sixth to Fifty Dollars More in the "Mackeson."

According to lines 8–14, which of the following is true?

a Four horses jumped the third-last fence close together.
b All five horses jumped the third-last fence together.
c Four horses almost collided at the third-last jump.

3a What was the name of the horse that took 2nd place in the King George VI Chase?

b What was the name of the horse that won the 'Mackeson'?

4 What were the two preconceived ideas mentioned in the first paragraph?

5 Now look at the start of this ice hockey report.

ICE HOCKEY

An abundance of goals helped to rewrite the record books at the weekend.

Complete this sentence:

The opening of the report prepares you to read about a lot of _____ and some new _____.

6 Here is the rest of the first paragraph.

> Murray-
> field's Derek Riley scored the
> 850th of his career to set a new
> target for British League
> strikers and help his team beat
> the Ayr Bruins 11-8, while Ted
> Phillips collected a hat-trick as
> Cleveland beat Altrincham 12-
> 4 to take his total to 100 in 50
> games for the North-east club.

What new records were set?

7 The next paragraph begins like this:

> Altrincham have now been
> defeated twice since losing
> their 12-game winning streak,
> but Dundee

Do you expect to read that Dundee won or lost their match?

8 The full paragraph follows.

> Altrincham have now been
> defeated twice since losing
> their 12-game winning streak,
> but Dundee continued their
> progress at the top with an 11-
> 9 victory over Fife. Al LeBlanc
> dominated for the champions,
> scoring seven and getting two
> assists.

What previous events are referred to in the first sentence?

9 Who does Al LeBlanc play for?

10 Which of the following phrases is most likely to introduce the next paragraph?

    a At that end of the table
    b At the other end of the table
    c At the top of the table

11 Here is the rest of the report.

> ------------------------------------
> Richmond stay one point off
> the relegation zone despite los-
> ing 17-5 to Blackpool and 11-1
> to Whitley. Dave Walsh scored
> four times for Blackpool and
> Peter Smith did the same for
> Whitley.
>
> For consistency, though,
> Southampton cannot be bet-
> tered. The Vikings' 9-6 defeat
> by Blackpool means they have
> lost 15 in a row.

How many goals did Smith score for Whitley?

12 Where do the 'Vikings' come from?

13 Which combination of words gives the last paragraph an ironical tone?

Section 4 Making reporting interesting 1

It is difficult to make sports reports varied. There are only a limited number of things that can happen in a game. This Section looks at how sports reporters still manage to make their writing interesting.

1 In a football match there are two possible results: one team beats the other, or there is a draw. It would become very boring if these results were always reported in the same words.

The extracts below are all summaries of football results. Read the extracts and decide whether the result was a win or a draw in each case.

Complete the table by writing W after each winning team, and D if it was a draw.

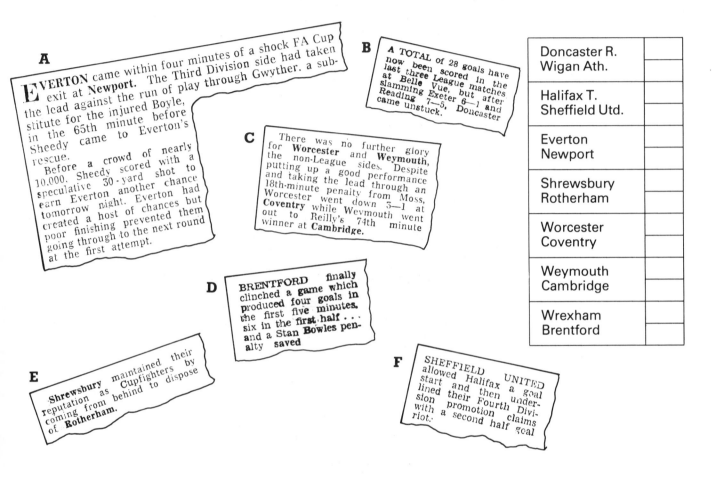

A EVERTON came within four minutes of a shock FA Cup exit at Newport. The Third Division side had taken the lead against the run of play through Gwyther, a substitute for the injured Boyle, in the 65th minute before Sheedy came to Everton's rescue.
Before a crowd of nearly 10,000, Sheedy scored with a speculative 30-yard shot to earn Everton another chance tomorrow night. Everton had created a host of chances but poor finishing prevented them going through to the next round at the first attempt.

B A TOTAL of 28 goals have now been scored in the last three League matches at Belle Vue, but after slamming Exeter 6—1 and Reading 7—5, Doncaster came unstuck.

C There was no further glory for **Worcester** and **Weymouth**, the non-League sides. Despite putting up a good performance and taking the lead through an 18th-minute penalty from Moss, Worcester went down 5—1 at **Coventry** while Weymouth went out to Reilly's 74th minute winner at **Cambridge**.

D BRENTFORD finally clinched a game which produced four goals in the first five minutes, six in the first half . . . and a Stan Bowles penalty saved

E Shrewsbury maintained their reputation as Cupfighters by coming from behind to dispose of **Rotherham**.

F SHEFFIELD UNITED allowed Halifax a goal start and then underlined their Fourth Division promotion claims with a second half goal riot.

Doncaster R. Wigan Ath.	
Halifax T. Sheffield Utd.	
Everton Newport	
Shrewsbury Rotherham	
Worcester Coventry	
Weymouth Cambridge	
Wrexham Brentford	

2 The italicised words below can all be used to report a team's victory, but some of them mean the team only just won and others mean that they won decisively.

Complete the table by writing in the words which refer to a decisive victory. (Use a dictionary to help you if necessary.)

Liverpool *crushed* Manchester.
Manchester *devastated* Liverpool.
Liverpool *hammered* Manchester.
Manchester *pipped* Liverpool.
Liverpool *scraped home* against Manchester.
Manchester *sneaked a win* against Liverpool.
Liverpool *thrashed* Manchester.
Manchester *trounced* Liverpool.
Liverpool *won by a mile* against Manchester.
Manchester *won by a whisker* against Liverpool.

Decisive victory

3 This exercise deals with the variety of ways in which the stages in the scoring have been reported.

Here are the reports of six football matches.

A

Berwick Rangers ......
Carlisle United ....

TWO GOALS in a 15 minute burst in the dying stages gave newly promoted Second Division Carlisle victory over Berwick Rangers

Inside forward Alan Shoulder broke the deadlock in 70 minutes crashing a low drive home from a Staniforth corner, then in 85 minutes, winger Caughlin slotted home number two.

But until then, apart from a brief flurry early on, it was the Scottish squad who were the more impressive.

B

Wolverh'pton W   Manchester C
Thrashed by Liverpool on Saturday, Manchester City were devastated at Molineux. Relegation-haunted Wolves looked more like a side searching for Europe in a first half which saw them four goals in 17 minutes.

Their best player was the veteran Hibbitt, who opened up the City defence in embarrassing fashion and crowned his performance with a goal from a swerving free kick. Gray, Clarke, and Eves added the others. City tightened up in the second half but all they could muster was a goal in the 76th minute by McDonald.

C

Sunderland   Birmingham C
Colin West, a 19-year-old striker who has spent most of the season in the reserves, helped Sunderland off the bottom of the first division with two first half goals. He opened the scoring in the 29th minute after Clarke headed against the bar. His second was set up by a buckley flick.

Birmingham had the better of the second half, but the nearest they came to scoring was in the 76th minute when McDowell missed an easy chance. They also had Broadhurst Stevenson booked, while Buckley was cautioned for Sunderland.

D

Stockport C. ....
Hull C. ....

LES MUTRIE hit a superb solo goal, his 27th of the season, and could afford to squander a couple of sitters

Steve McLaren put City ahead after 12 minutes and Mutrie, collecting a long ball from Neil Thompson, made an exhibition of the second 10 minutes after the interval.

Osher Williams pulled a goal back when Hull's defenders hesitated in chasing a bouncing ball. Williams darted in, headed against the bar and bundled the rebound over the line.

E

Rochdale ....
York C. ....

YORK'S Peter Aitken was sent off or appealing too strongly against the second half penalty that put the final nail in his side's coffin.

Eugene Martinez put lowly Rochdale ahead when he hammered home a corner after 18 minutes.

Rochdale made sure of the points when Bill Williams was fouled by Laverick and Wellings scored from the spot

F

Darlington ....
Hartlepool ....

A SPARKLING four-goal second half show by Alan Walsh transformed the 100th derby between these two old North East rivals.

Hartlepool raced into a two-goal lead through Alan Harding and Harry Clark, but Darlington pulled one back before half-time when David McLean headed home a Roger Wicks free kick.

And then came the Walsh broadside. He equalised a minute after the interval with a 25-yard shot, got his second from the penalty spot after 67 minutes and completed his hat-trick two minutes later with another long-range shot.

David Speedie crossed for Walsh to head his fourth in the last minute.

Underline the phrases in the reports that mean the same as the following:

a ended a situation where neither side was winning.
(report A)
b scored so that one team took the lead.
(reports D and E)
c reduced the lead by one goal.
(reports D and F)
d scored so that both teams had the same number of goals.
(report F)
e three goals scored by one player.
(report F)

4 The scores are missing from the tops of the reports. Read the reports and complete the results by adding the scores to each one.

5 The main activity in football is kicking the ball, but it would soon become boring if the activity was always described in the same way. In fact, the word 'kick' is rarely used in football reporting except in phrases such as 'free kick', or when one player kicks another. Instead of 'kicking' the ball into the goal or to another player, a footballer is reported to 'pass' the ball, to 'chip it in' or to 'slam it home' etc.

In the space below list the words and phrases in the reports above which have been used instead of 'a kick', 'kicked' and 'kicking'.

6 As you saw in Section 1 of this Unit (page 61), it is common for sports reporters to place additional information in front of nouns.

a Circle the three pieces of extra information given in this way about teams in reports A, B and E.

b If the reporters had not been trying to use an economical style, they might have written this information differently. From the phrases below, choose the one which corresponds best to each of the pieces of information you have circled.

   a who have just moved down to a lower division
   b who have just moved up from a lower division
   c who are in a much lower position
   d who are at the top of the division
   e who are hoping to move up to a higher division
   f who are in danger of being moved down to a lower division

7 How does the writer of report A refer to the final part of the game?

8 According to report B, were Manchester City more convincingly beaten at Liverpool or Wolverhampton?

9 Report C says that McDowell 'missed an easy chance'. A similar situation is described in report D. What phrase is used here to mean 'to miss some easy chances'.

10 It is not always possible for a reporter to be original—for example, when reporting the technical details of the game, such as the rules and the consequences of breaking them.

This exercise deals with cases where the rules are broken. In the spaces below, write words or phrases used in the reports which mean the same as the following:

a One player trips or kicks another. (E)	
b The referee gives a player a warning about his behaviour. (C)	
c The referee records a player's name for misbehaviour. (C)	
d The referee tells a player to leave the pitch for an offence. (E)	

11 Of the words you listed in question 5, 'crash', 'hammer' and 'drive' all indicate forceful kicking. The words below can all be used to replace the verb 'kick'. Which ones would be used to describe forceful kicking? (Use a dictionary to help with this exercise if necessary.)

clout	nudge	rap	tap	thump
guide	ram	roll	thud	touch

Section 5 Making reporting interesting 2

This Section looks at the way sports reporters choose particularly emotional and descriptive language to bring their reports to life.

1 On the next page are two versions of the same report on an exciting football match between Motherwell and Celtic. The one on the left has been altered. All the words chosen by the writer to bring the report to life have been replaced by the more neutral words in italics.

The reporter's original words are listed below. Complete the report on the right by inserting the reporter's words in the appropriate places.

Version 1

This was Celtic's *best*
performance in years.
They looked *better*
from the start, and once the scoring
began, in the 29th minute, the gap
between the sides *increased considerably*.
Nicholas hit a hat-trick; McGarvey's
goal was the best of the lot; and
Danny McGrain seldom could have
turned in a *better* performance.
From the kick off, Celtic *attacked*
Sproat's goal with Provan in *great*
form but Motherwell defended in the
uncompromising style one associates
with teams managed by Jock Wallace,
conceding ten free kicks in as many
minutes.

Version 2

This was Celtic's *a* _____
performance in years.
They looked *b* _____
from the start, and once the scoring
began, in the 29th minute, the gap
between the sides *c* _____
_____.
Nicholas hit a hat-trick; McGarvey's
goal was the best of the lot; and
Danny McGrain seldom could have
turned in a *d* _____ performance.
From the kick off, Celtic *e* _____
Sproat's goal with Provan in *f* _____
form but Motherwell defended in the
uncompromising style one associates
with teams managed by Jock Wallace,
conceding ten free kicks in as many
minutes.

Reporter's original words

dazzling
more flawlessly majestic
most devastating
pounded
rapidly widened to embarrassing
    proportions
vastly superior

2   Which version do you prefer?

3   It is probably easier to make the report of a good match interesting to read. But sports writers have to report a lot of bad matches too.

Look at the report below.

Tottenham Hotspur ... 1	Swansea City 0
by Brian Glanville	

BY ONE of those ironies in which football is so rich, Swansea had their solitary decent shot of this drab game at the very moment the referee mercifully blew the final whistle. James hit it well, Clemence turned it round the post; a fine drive, a fine save. But had Swansea equalised, what a farce it would have been.

We had to endure 35 minutes of absolute nothingness, during which the most exciting moment was when a man was called over the loudspeakers to the hospital where his wife had just presented him with twins, then, blessedly, a goal arrived. Tottenham scored it, and it was an unexpectedly good one.

Underline the words and combinations of words that make the reporting interesting but show at the same time that the game was not good.

4   The table opposite should contain eight pairs of words. Each pair refers to the same aspect of a player's style or behaviour, but one indicates a positive view of it and the other indicates a negative view.

For example, 'confident' and 'arrogant' could both be used to describe a player who knows that he is good. But 'confident' shows that the reporter takes a positive view of this characteristic, whilst 'arrogant' shows that the reporter takes a negative view.

Read the list of words below and write them into the appropriate spaces to complete the table that follows. (Use a dictionary to do this exercise if necessary.)

adventurous	confident	inexperienced	predictable
casual	conventional	ostentatious	selfish

Positive	Negative
confident	arrogant
consistent	
	reckless
youthful	
	boring
individualistic	
	careless
flamboyant	

Section 6 Making reporting interesting 3

This Section looks at some other ways sports writers use language to maintain interest in their reporting.

1 Look at the first line of this extract.

> DEFEAT and aftermath: seeing all the frailties and few of the strengths. The hopelessness. The humiliation.

If you did not know that it had appeared on a sports page, what would you expect the rest of the article to be about?

2 Here is the rest of the extract.

> There is no more painful place in the world for England to lose at cricket than in Australia. and when they fail to even make a close game of it, then they get a verbal mugging from The Hill. where bodies sizzle on the outside and are sozzled with cold beer on the inside.

a What does the choice of this style tell you about the writer's attitude to cricket?

b Why does the writer feel that despair is particularly justified in this case?

c What would be the effect of this style on a reader who did not share the writer's attitude to the sport?

When a match is dull or its result is disappointing the reporter must work hard to keep his/her readers interested. S/he may use a style which is more common in other situations—in the case of the writer above, a highly dramatic style.

---

3 The writer of the following report also uses language which is more commonly found in a different situation. It concerns a one-sided rugby game on New Year's Day between the Army and the Harlequins.

Few citations as Army are easily outgunned

By DOUG IBBOTSON

Harlequins .... 42pts   Army 6

ON the evidence of manœuvres against Harlequins at the Stoop Memorial Ground on Saturday the Army must seriously re-examine both basic training and personnel before taking on the
5 Navy at Twickenham in March.

Beaten by a goal, six tries, three penalties and a dropped goal to a single goal the Army
10 were often as irresolute in defence and impotent in attack as the margin suggests.

In working off their seasonal excesses during a dull first half,
15 Harlequins established a 15-point platform from which to launch imaginative training moves under something akin to match conditions.

20 They proved effective enough for full-back Dudman to score his 100th point of the season and — when he added a dropped goal to three penalties and a
25 conversion — his 14th of the afternoon.

Butcher scored three tries, Woodhouse two and forwards Oliver and Weekes one each as
30 the Army's heavy infantry were outclassed and the cavalry seldom appeared.

Look at the headline to this report. Why would **Few praised as army are easily beaten** have been a less effective headline?

4 Line 31 refers to the cavalry. In the old cowboy tradition, which of the following is usually associated with the appearance of the cavalry?

   a attack
   b disaster
   c rescue
   d speed

5 Underline the places where the reporter borrows language more usually used in a military context.

6 The following reports also borrow language from other areas. Read the reports and underline the borrowed language in each case. For each report make a note of the context in which the language is more commonly found.

A GOLF

It was like chasing a Ferrari in Chevrolets, said Tom Kite, and if we continue in the racing idiom it might be added that most of the pursuers blew up their engines in the vain attempt to stop Severiano Ballesteros winning his second Masters.

B TABLE TENNIS

Like Grand National hopefuls, all nine England players cleared their first-round fences at the 37th World Championships in Tokyo yesterday, but there are likely to be several fallers today when the going gets tougher.

C Athletics

ALBERTO SALAZAR, the marathon's unbeaten American king, goes to a muddy field in Gateshead this weekend to settle a score which has nothing to do with the Australian claimant to his throne, Rob de Castella.

E RUGBY UNION

David Foot — Bath 27, Royal Navy 13

Navy go down in Bath

Bath recovered from a tentative start, got wise to the Navy's energetic and, at times, adventurous approach and becalmed them systematically to win by three goals and three penalties to a goal, a try and a penalty.

D SOCCER

Like Italian politics, the balance of power in the relegation region alters almost daily. Before Saturday, having come through five unbeaten games, Brighton were contemplating another year in a First Division seat; after it, with their loss compounded by gains for Luton and Norwich, their standing in the polls has fallen sharply.

Section 7 Appealing to the interests and attitudes of the reader

Like other news reporters, sports writers choose their style and focus with a particular sort of reader in mind.

1   The extracts below are the opening paragraphs from three different reports of the same football match. The game was between Arsenal and Leeds and the score was 1–1.

A "COME ON ARSENAL, I haven't got the fare to go to Leeds," cried one fan as the Gunners could only scramble a draw against the visitors' massed defence superbly marshalled by Leeds player-manager Eddie Gray.

B HISTORY, as far as Arsenal – Leeds matches go, seems to repeat itself, first as 0–0 draws, than as 1–1 draws. This—the fourteenth such result in 79 meetings—was neither tragedy nor farce, containing very little drama of any kind. In fact, it was so sterile that the only comment Arsenal manager Terry Neill could provide was that this was typical Cup football, with very little decent football.

C LEEDS' abrasive defence yesterday stifled any Arsenal originality to earn a deserved if unexpected re-play.

a   Which report would you choose to read if you wanted the following:

  a   an analysis of the game.   (report   )
  b   a brief summary of the game.   (report   )

b   What sort of details would you get from the other report?

2   Here are the descriptions of the goals from the same three reports.

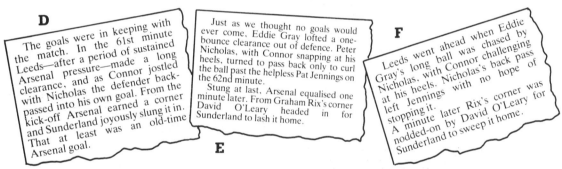

D The goals were in keeping with the match. In the 61st minute Leeds—after a period of sustained Arsenal pressure—made a long clearance, and as Connor jostled with Nicholas the defender back-passed into his own goal. From the kick-off Arsenal earned a corner and Sunderland joyously slung it in. That at least was an old-time Arsenal goal.

E Just as we thought no goals would ever come, Eddie Gray lofted a one-bounce clearance out of defence. Peter Nicholas, with Connor snapping at his heels, turned to pass back only to curl the ball past the helpless Pat Jennings on the 62nd minute.
    Stung at last, Arsenal equalised one minute later. From Graham Rix's corner David O'Leary headed in for Sunderland to lash it home.

F Leeds went ahead when Eddie Gray's long ball was chased by Nicholas, with Connor challenging at his heels. Nicholas's back pass left Jennings with no hope of stopping it.
    A minute later Rix's corner was nodded-on by David O'Leary for Sunderland to sweep it home.

Which description belongs with each report?

3   The two articles which follow on the next page report on a marathon race.

a   Which of the following details would *you* hope to read about in a report on a marathon race? Tick your answers in the first column of the table below.

		G	H
a	The name of the winner.		
b	The winner's time.		
c	The fastest woman.		
d	The fastest woman's time.		
e	News of any international or national records broken.		
f	News of any personal best times achieved.		
g	Reports on the weather.		
h	Reports on the numbers and attitudes of spectators.		

b Which of those details appear in each of the following articles? Put your answers in the other two columns of the table.

G

Mike Gratton, from the Invicta Club in Kent, and Gerry Helme, from St Helens in Lancashire, brought a hint
5 of quality back to British marathon running in the Gillette London race yesterday. Together with Hugh Jones, the winner of last year's race, they
10 go to Helsinki in August to represent Britain in the World Championships.
Gratton became Amateur Athletic Association champion
15 and Britain's third fastest man at the distance behind Ian Thompson (2hr 9min 12 sec in 1974) and Jones (2hr 9min 24 sec last year) with his time of
20 2hr 9min 44 sec, a personal improvement of 2min 22 sec. Helme, with 2 hr 10min 12 sec, went better by over 4½ minutes. It is a long time since
25 British runners made an impact at international level in this event. Thompson's double victory in the Commonwealth Games and European Cham-
30 pionships is nine years ago and before that it was Ron Hill in the European Championships in Athens in 1969. Yesterday, in his 70th marathon, Hill
35 finished in 2hr 23 min 47 sec.
He was advocating last week that the solid army of British marathon runners — 50 men finished inside 2 hours 16min
40 30 sec yesterday — should be taking a closer look at the quality of their training rather than the quantity. The obsession with mileage must be re-
45 sisted. The first two home showed, one by design and the other by accident, that this is the way to catch the Salazars and de Castellas.

H

A SLATE grey and drizzly day produced perfect conditions for the 18,000 competi-
5 tors, in the London marathon yesterday. There were many personal best times and an equal world women's record for the Norwegian Grete Waitz.
10 Tens of thousands of Londoners spurned the weather to line the route from Greenwich Park to Westminster
15 Bridge beneath a sea of multicoloured umbrellas. Ms Waitz, her blonde pony tail snapping in the wind, crossed the line in 2 hours,
20 25 minutes and 29 seconds. She was 14 minutes behind the winner, Michael Gratton, from Canterbury, who strode to the tape with apparently effortless ease.

4 Look at article G. Match each group of names on the left with one of the sentences on the right.

1 Gratton, Jones, Thompson	a They are Britain's fastest marathon runners.
2 Hill, Thompson	b They will run the marathon for Britain in the World Athletics Championships.
3 Gratton, Helme, Jones	c They are British runners who have been successful in international marathons.

5a Who does 'he' (line 36) refer to?

b Who are 'the solid army of British marathon runners' (lines 37–38)?

c Who does 'the first two home' (line 45) refer to?

6 What do you think follows line 49?

a Details of the training programmes of the first two home.
b Details of the running styles of Salazar and de Castella.
c Details of how athletes can increase mileage in their training programmes.

7a Complete the table below to show the contrasting styles of the two articles.

Information		
The fact that some runners broke their own records.	a 'a personal improvement of 2 min. 22 sec.' (G) b (G)	(H)
The first mention of Michael Gratton.	(G)	(H)
Details of the winner's time.	(G)	(H)

b Label the two columns to show what the contrast is. Choose the headings from the following list.

- *a* Descriptive / Neutral
- *b* Emotional / Neutral
- *c* Exaggeration / Understatement
- *d* Humorous / Serious
- *e* Technical / Non-technical

8 How would the style of article H be different if it started like this:

'A wet and overcast day produced favourable conditions for the 18,000 competitors in the London marathon yesterday.'

9a Why isn't Grete Waitz mentioned in article G?

b In article H, she is mentioned in lines 8–9 and 16–19. Comment on the details that have been chosen for reporting.

10 Here are three quotations recorded after the race.

J | 'Tonight I'm going to get drunk.'

K | 'I feel knackered but I'm just pleased to have finished a marathon.'

L | 'I knew I had pushed out a gap of about 30 metres but I wasn't improving on it and there was always the fear that Gerry might come back.'

a Which of these quotations does not come from Michael Gratton?

b Of the two quotations that are from Michael Gratton, which one is likely to be reported in article G?

11 Which of the following headlines belongs with each article?

M Runners leave troubles behind

N GRATTON PROVES A POINT OF QUALITY

12 Who are each of these articles intended to appeal to?

G _____

H _____

APPENDIX
Further suggestions for the classroom use of newspapers

The topical nature of the press means that newspapers present themselves as an obvious and stimulating starting point for discussion. But their exploitation in the classroom need not be restricted to this alone. The suggestions below will hopefully encourage teachers to experiment more widely with newspapers in the classroom. Those of the exercises which appear in the book were designed to help students to read newspapers. But this list also includes activities with wider purposes so that newspapers can be incorporated into the general work of the class. They involve a variety of skills, but concentrate mainly on reading and specifically:

skimming	—reading for gist
scanning	—reading for specific information
interpretation	—reading for implication, to distinguish fact from opinion etc.
prediction	—anticipating what is to come
guessing	—deducing the meaning of unknown elements from context

Where there are examples of particular exercises in this book, a reference is given—

e.g. (1/1/4/p.12)	which means	Unit I, Section 1, question 4 on page 12.

Activities using the contents and layout of a newspaper

1 Comparing coverage

In small groups or pairs, or individually for homework, the students are asked to complete a tally showing how the contents of a paper break down into Foreign/Home News, Comment, Features, pictures etc. (They may be given a check list.) This involves skimming and can become more interesting if different groups examine different newspapers and then compare and discuss the results.

2 Search quiz

Students are asked in advance to buy and bring to class a copy of a particular newspaper. The teacher devises a number of questions—at least 20—based on the contents of that paper. Individually or in pairs the students work through the newspaper, locating the required information. Mainly a reading activity, this exercise can be varied to cater for different levels. In a simplified version the questions would require a search of headlines or first paragraphs. A more sophisticated activity would involve a more detailed search of full articles, or the use of cryptic clues.

In a final variation which also involves writing, the students are asked to buy different newspapers and then compose their own questions for their classmates.

3 Compiling a news programme

The students are divided into groups and each group is given a newspaper or a selection of about 20 articles from one or several newspapers. They then have to select about ten articles, shorten and adapt them for oral presentation, arrange them in order of importance, and then read them into a tape recorder, producing a news broadcast which is finally played to the other groups. This involves them in a wide range of speaking, reading, writing and listening skills and a lot of co-operative activity.

Activities using newspaper headlines

These exercises provide practice in:

1 Understanding the language of headlines

a The headlines are removed from a series of short articles, jumbled up and listed. The students match headlines to articles. If the headlines contain words from the articles, the task involves scanning. Otherwise interpretation is required. (1/1/4/p.12) Alternatively, with a single longer article, students can be asked to select a headline from several alternatives. The distractors can be incorrect from a factual, attitudinal or stylistic point of view. (4/1/15/p.51)

b Two or more articles—or parts of articles, such as first paragraphs—on the same story are collected. It is important that there should be some clearly distinguishable difference in style or focus. The headlines are removed and the students match them to the correct articles. (2/4/3/p.32)

c One word is removed from the headline and the students supply it after reading the article. The word which is removed could, if the students are sufficiently advanced, involve a play on words. (1/1/1 p.11)

2 Using headlines to predict content, style and attitude

a A headline is chosen and students use it to predict the content, style or attitude of the article. A multiple choice or open-ended format can be used. Longer headlines are more suitable for exercises on prediction of content—distractors should be based on the possible misinterpretations of the simplified style of long headlines (1/3/1/p.15). For examples using shorter headlines (1/4/p.16).

b A headline with a play on words is selected. Students are given definitions of all the possible interpretations of the words which make up the headline and try to guess the content of the article from which it comes. Alternatively, they can be asked to suggest as many stories as possible that the headline would be appropriate for.

Activities using newspaper articles

These exercises provide practice in:

1 Handling unfamiliar vocabulary

a Students are asked to identify a word or phrase in an article on the basis of a definition, a synonym, an antonym or some other clue. Providing the word given is not more obscure than the target word or phrase this can encourage contextualised guessing. (4/4/3/p.57)

b A word is identified and students asked to guess its general meaning by using the context. If a multiple choice format is used the distractors should all be approximate rather than exact meanings—e.g. 'mudflats are a kind of land'—testing the students' awareness of the function of the word in the text rather than its dictionary definition. (2/3/4/p.30)

c A word is identified. Students are presented with several possible meanings and select the one which is appropriate to the context. (2/3/3/p.30)

2 Processing information

a A series of statements relating to an article are presented and students judge each of them true or false according to the article. The exercise involves simple scanning or a greater degree of interpretation depending on whether or not paraphrasing has been used. The statements may relate to the implications of the article rather than its factual content. A variation is to include a third option—'the text doesn't say'. Students can also be asked to correct the incorrect statements. (4/3/12/p.56)

b Two or more articles which report the same story but cover different facts are selected. The students are given a checklist of factual details concerning the story. Their task is to scan the articles to find which, if any, of them contains the information. The details in the checklist can be paraphrased from the articles so that a greater degree of interpretation is required. (3/4/8/p.46) Alternatively, students may be asked to compile their own checklists of contents. This exercise can provide a good starting point for a discussion on the neutrality of the Press.

c A number of sentences are divided into two parts which are then jumbled up and listed. Students match the halves to reproduce the original sentences. (4/1/8/p.50) As an alternative students may be given one half of each sentence and asked to supply the second themselves. (4/2/2/p.51) These exercises can be used to check comprehension or, if grammatical constraints restrict the possible endings, as a grammar check, or finally as a check on students' awareness of style. They will also help to develop predictive skills.

d A text is divided up into self-contained sections (on the basis of paragraph divisions or other suitable criteria). Each section is numbered and given a heading which describes its contents as succinctly as possible. The headings are then jumbled and listed. The object of the exercise is, after having read the text, to match each heading to the appropriate numbered section. This practises skimming and scanning and can be used as a starting point for focusing on the organisation of the text. (4/5/1/p.58)

e A sentence or paragraph is removed at or towards the end of an article. It is then offered in multiple choice format as one of several possible endings. The students have to choose the most appropriate. The distractors can be incorrect from a factual or attitudinal point of view, encouraging the students to test various hypotheses about the overall conclusions of the article. Or they can be inappropriate from a stylistic point of view, encouraging students to take account of this variable. (2/4/7/p.33)

f Several articles or parts of articles are selected so that the students have a range of information in front of them. The pieces may cover different aspects or stages of the same story, or may simply be thematically related. The students answer questions by skimming and scanning across the variety of sources. Depending on how the questions are phrased, the students will be involved in varying degrees of interpretation. If thematically linked articles are chosen, the students can be asked to draw conclusions, make deductions, generalisations etc. on the basis of the information available to them. If extracts covering the same story are used, and if they contain clear clues as to their place in the sequence of events, students can be asked to organise them in chronological order. This also draws students' attention to the importance of organisational features such as reference and sequencing signals. (2/1/6/p.27)

g An article is physically reduced by cutting away the outside edges. The students are set comprehension questions which they have to answer by skimming and scanning, since it is physically impossible to pore over every word.

h The students extract information from an article, to complete a grid or table, or label a diagram. When completed this can be given to another student who reconstructs the text. The exercise involves scanning and writing.

i A number of incidents are taken from an article and listed in a different order from that in which they occurred. The students reorganise the list to show the correct sequence of events. (Alternatively an argument making a sequence of points may be used.) If the items in the list are paraphrased from the original, interpretation rather than simply scanning is involved. This activity can be used as a starting point for focusing on the organisation of the text.

j An article can be retyped so that it contains a number of extra phrases or sentences. The students detect which parts do not belong to the article. The additions can be inconsistent from a factual, attitudinal or stylistic point of view. In addition to requiring interpretation, this exercises the students' predictive techniques.

k The students are presented with a word, phrase or sentence from the text and have to supply the question that elicits it as an answer. This requires scanning, interpretation and grammar transformation. A more advanced variation is to supply students with synonyms or paraphrases instead of the exact words of the text.

l One in every ten or twelve words is deleted from an article—any more might be too difficult and any fewer too easy. The students supply the missing word or a suitable alternative. (Finding the exact word is an extremely demanding task, particularly with newspapers.) An alternative is to delete selected words, drawing attention to specific aspects of the text such as stylistic features, link words, prepositions etc. Both exercises become easier if a multiple choice format is used, with alternatives offered either at each blank or in a list at the end. (4/2/8/p.53) The exercise involves predictive reading.

3 Understanding the organisation of the information

a A text must be chosen where a number of reference words—e.g. *this*, *that*—are used. The references are listed, or in some other way identified, and the students find the person or thing to which each refers. Alternatively, students may be asked to identify for themselves all the references to one particular person or thing. (2/1/4/p.26) This activity encourages an awareness of the cohesion of the text.

b Three articles on the same text are selected and the organisation of each is summarised into headings. Students match each set of headings to the appropriate article. (3/4/1/p.43)

c An article which reveals a clear sequence of ideas or facts is divided into sections at the sentence or paragraph level. (Sports reports may be ideal for this.) The students reorder the sections to recreate the original article. The task will require interpretation and an awareness of the linguistic signals of reference, sequence, and the various relationships between ideas (e.g. *this*, *first*, *consequently*). (2/2/4/p.28)

d Every so often a phrase or sentence is removed from an article. It is important that the removal can be achieved without totally destroying the coherence of the article. The phrases/sentences are listed. Students can be asked to insert them into the text. A more advanced variation involves retyping the article to eliminate the spaces. Students then identify the point in the text where each item comes from. This exercise draws attention to the way sentences and ideas are related to one another. (4/5/10/p.60) e The headline, the first paragraph—and possibly the last paragraph and some key words—are taken from an article. It is important to choose an article where the first paragraph establishes the topic adequately and the last paragraph, if it is used, provides a summary. The task is to predict the rest of the article by choosing multiple choice alternatives on the likely content of the missing parts (3/5/5–6/p.47). A more advanced version would involve asking the students to write the missing part themselves.

f Exercise 2h above (page 78) can be extended by asking the student writing the text to alter the organisation or focus from that of the original in a specified way.

g An article is divided into five or six parts—it is important to choose a text which falls naturally into distinct sections. The class is divided into a similar number of groups, each group receiving one section of the text. The members of the groups all make notes on the contents of their section, trying to reach a consensus on the essential points. They try to estimate its position in the text as a whole—whether it is likely to be from the beginning, middle or end—and then they discuss the possible contents of the article. Using only their notes, the class then negotiate the reassembly of the article. The group believing themselves to have the first part of the article dictate their notes for the rest of the class to record. The group believing themselves to have the second piece follow. The procedure continues until all the groups have read out their notes and every class member has a satisfactory copy of them. It is important to have a chairperson in control of this to ensure its smooth running. This could be the teacher, but need not be. If the students are autonomous, their judges will be their peers and their success will be determined by the extent to which they are understood. The class then goes on to discuss whether or not the correct order has been established, and when agreement is reached each student attempts to rewrite the summary in full. This activity involves a range of speaking, reading, writing and listening skills.

4 Understanding stylistic features

a Exercise 2h above can be extended by asking the student writing the text to alter the style from that of the original in a specified way.

b Certain words or phrases are identified and students are asked to select those which correspond in meaning but which indicate stylistic variation. (2/3/13/p 31)

c The first paragraphs of two or more stylistically different articles covering the same story are taken and students are asked to match these extracts with later paragraphs from the same articles. (5/7/2/p.73)

d A more sophisticated task involves asking students to identify words or phrases which have a particular stylistic function, and to make stylistic comparisons between different articles. As an introduction to this kind of activity students may be asked to make comparisons between a stylistically loaded piece—one that is particularly conversational, descriptive or emotional—and a neutral version of it written in standard English by the teacher. (2/4/5/p.33)

Activities using the rest of the newspaper

1 Letters

a *Answering*   Students can reply to letters on topical points.

b *Debate*   Letters can be collected over a period of a few days and the students can be given them as an aid to marshalling arguments and ideas for a debate or discussion.

c *Reconstruction*   All the responses to a letter can be collected and given to the students. They then have to reconstruct the original letter from what is contained in the replies.

A Advertisements

a *Slogans*   Slogans are collected from commercial advertisements. Students discuss them and attempt to establish what is being advertised in each case. They are then given copies of the original advertisements, minus slogans, and have to match them with the slogans.

b *Claims*   Students can be asked to distinguish facts from claims, discuss the appeal of the advertisement and what makes it effective.

c *Small ads*   Students can be asked to skim and scan small ads, entertainment guides etc. for specific information.

3 Cartoons

a The captions can be removed from a number of cartoons, jumbled up and listed. The students have to match the captions to the cartoons.

b The speech bubbles are removed from several frames of a cartoon strip. The students then have to match the bubbles to the frames.

c   The speech is removed from the speech bubbles in some but not all frames of a cartoon strip. The students have to suggest what the characters might be saying.

4 Puzzles

Crosswords, word puzzles etc. can be done for their own sake, although some simplification of the rules may sometimes be necessary. Other alterations may also be desirable. For example, 'Spot the difference' puzzles could be more usefully done in the language classroom if the differences between the two pictures were established through verbal description and questioning rather than on the basis of visual comparison.

ANSWER KEY

Unit 1

Section 1

1. A Jobs *boost* for new town   B Cider *boom*   C Safety *plea*   D Sugar pay *deal*   E Yacht *tragedy*   F Press *curb*   G Ski *ordeal*   H Bangladesh *aid*   I Car *blast*   J Cheese *haul*   K £200m *blow*   L Big *drive* for cough jabs   M Air record *bid*   N Bomb *scare*

2. *a* remove   *b* reject   *c* propose   *d* acquire

3. *a* take up   *b* come across   *c* build up   *d* blow up

4. A Poison all-clear   B Fire-bomb riddle   C Hospital rap   D Cruelty probe   E Blaze terror   F Death probe   G Blaze victim   H Corpse horror   I Death plunge   J Killer bug's new victims   K Bomb haul   L Poison peril

5. *a* look at   *b* look into   *c* come across   *d* get away

6. It would make the articles more conversational.

Section 2

1. A Driver *quizzed*   B 9,700 *flee* floods   C Waiter *held*   D Firm *to axe* 1,900   E Cycle fares *cut* by BR   F Strike *hits* travellers   G Bridge *to go* (*goes* is also possible)   H Lambeth *snubs* card system   I Bite *bars* record   J Building activity *to be boosted*

Section 3

1. A *c*   B *a*   C *b*   D *b*   E *a*   F *c*   G *b*   H *c*

2. *a* British Broadcasting Corporation   *b* British Rail   *c* Civil Aviation Authority   *d* Confederation of British Industry   *e* Criminal Investigation Department   *f* European Economic Community   *g* Football Association   *h* Independent Television   *i* Member of Parliament (also Military Police)   *j* National Health Service   *k* Police Constable   *l* Physical Training   *m* Royal Society for the Prevention of Cruelty to Animals   *n* Trades Union Congress   *o* United Kingdom

Section 4

1. *a* 'Boom' leads you to expect something positive.
   b 'Boost' leads you to expect something positive.
   c 'Soar' leads you to expect a dramatic increase.
   d 'Threat' leads you to expect something negative.
   e 'Looms' leads you to expect something negative.

2a. A
   b. It is more important to know the number involved—it is assumed that the report concerns people and not dogs. If there was something special about the people—for example, if they were nurses—the headline might be 'Salmonella kills nurses' or 'Salmonella kills three nurses', depending on what the reporter felt was most important. (*Note* If only one person is involved, the number is already contained in the noun, e.g. 'girl', 'nurse', 'dancer' etc.)

3. D

4. F

5. G

Section 5

1. A *Snap*, lads!   B *Blast* it!   C Steve *cracks* it   D Prison *record*

2. gag   pun   wisecrack   witticism

3. *Across:* 1 Deal   2 Park   3 Reel   5 Trip   6 Cast   8 Mean
   Down: 1 Duck   2 Poor   4 Last   6 Clip   7 Neat   9 Loom

Section 6

1. A Window (pane) *pain*   B Twisted

(tail) *tale*   C (plain) *Plane* crazy
D (some) *Sum* hope. (In fact, because of
English understatement the phrase
'Some hope' on its own usually means
there is little or no hope.)

2   *Across: 1* Maid   *2* Made   *3* Scent
4 Sent   *5* Minor   *6* Miner   *7* Feat
8 Feet   *9* Hole   *10* Whole   *11* Steal
12 Steel   *13* Hair   *14* Hare   *15* Sail
16 Sale
Down: 1 Meet   *5* Meat   *9* Heel   *13* Heal

Section 7

1   A Happy   B Sore   C Hell   D Raw

Section 8

1   A *Denture* venture   B Crane *strain*
C *Wing*-ding

2   *a* went off   *b* went against   *c* went
over   *d* went on   *e* went for

3   It would make the sentences more
formal.

4   A Charity *chop*   B Snake *snag*
C Quads *quandary*

5   *a*

6   *a* retired   *b* rejected   *c* arrived
d approached   *e* refused entry

7   It makes them less formal.

Unit 2

Section 1

1a   A is the first report.
b   Look at the box which follows the
question.

2   F

3   'Stephen Waldorf, who was the
mistaken victim of a shooting
incident, . . .'/'Stephen Waldorf,
who was shot when mistaken for
another man, . . .' or something
similar.

4   H

5   There were previous offences.

6   *1* I   *2* F   *3* J   *4* E   *5* G   *6* C
7 H   *8* D
(To arrive at this order, it is necessary
to accept that 'last week' (G) refers to a
more recent incident than '11 days
ago' (C).)

7   *c*

8   It gives it a double meaning. 'Ringing'
is associated with bells. 'Ringing up'
is associated with a shopkeeper's cash
register. It combines romance and
commercialism, which is what the
Bank's scheme also does.

Section 2

1   *b*

2   *a*

3   *a*

4   *1* A   *2* E   *3* C   *4* D   *5* G   *6* H
7 F   *8* B

5   push—hustle   shut—slam
break—smash

6   attack—have a go at

7   Because they are large animals and the
results were the same as if the house
had been deliberately wrecked.

8a and b
Eating

bolt	hastily without chewing
chew	work with the teeth
crunch	crush noisily with teeth
gnaw	bite again and again
gobble	hurriedly and noisily
gulp	greedily or with effort
nibble	taking small bites
slurp	noisily

Drinking

down	swallow quickly without tasting
gulp	greedily or with effort
sip	taking small mouthfuls
slurp	noisily
swig	large mouthfuls

Section 3

1   Because 'flutter' is associated with the
movement of wings.

2   'Bird-watchers' is less formal and so
goes better with the conversational
style of 'set . . . a-flutter'.

3   *c*

4   *c*

5   *a*

6   *b*

7a   the Tees estuary (line 26)
b   visitor (headline), one of Britain's
rarest feathered visitors (lines 5–6), (a
long-toed stint, a member of the sandpiper family (lines 8–10)), it (line 12),
the 6-inch chestnut and white wader
with distinctive white eyebrows and
abnormally long feet (lines 21–24),
It (line 29).

8   The chestnut and white wader is six
inches long. It has distinctive white
eyebrows and abnormally long feet.

9   Wader joins birds on Tees sanctuary.

10   *c*

11   *b*

12 *a*

13

	Technical
space-man	astronaut
map-maker	cartographer
weather-man	meteorologist
woman-hater	misogynist
eye specialist	ophthalmologist

Section 4

1   Headline A: It is impossible to tell what the writer thinks of it.
Headline B: The writer thinks it is a bad thing.

2   The language of headline A is neutral. 'Scandal' and 'slave' in headline B are emotional.

3   A D
B C

4   *b* Quoting someone else's words: A
e Drawing attention to the writer's use of a nickname or special term: B

5   *a* swooped *b* battered *c* provocative
d brutal *e* volatile *f* incensed
g stormed *h* dragged *i* dragged
j armed with *k* slashed
(*c* and *d* could be the other way round, but the order above is better.)

6   Horror at the police behaviour; sympathy for the residents of Brixton. The words you put into the second version are all emotional, showing the writer's attitude.

7   *c* (*a* is too neutral. *b* is sympathetic to the police and not the people of Brixton.)

Section 5

1

Descriptive and conversational	*Formal and neutral*
ganged up on the referee (article B)	a football referee was assaulted (article A)
their team was thrashed 6–1 (article B)	whose team had just lost a match by 6–1 (article A)

2   To make it clear that it is referring to the referee of that particular game.

3   A C
B D

4   F

5   E LGJ
F IHK

6   The use of 'never again' as a summary of his exact words, and the use of 'crook' instead of the more formal 'criminal'.

7   *a* advertisement *b* doctor
c husband *d* laboratory
f representative *g* reverend
h vegetable(s) *i* veterinarian
j wellington boot

Section 6

1   Humurous

2   'Boiled over' could also refer to what happened to the car's engine. It therefore has a double meaning.

3   A wounded animal

4   It would be less descriptive, saying nothing about the speed of the movement, or the man's mood.

5   breaking the windows
hitting

6   *a*

7a This could mean any car.
 b The writer wants to emphasise the surprising fact that the driver was wrecking his own car.

8   The reporter gets a more dramatic effect.

9   *b*—one car doesn't make a scrap-yard.

10 Because he had taken out his anger on the car and was now quite calm.

11 attacked it

12 It is a play on words. 'Carnage' means destruction in a disaster or a battle. The hyphen draws attention to the word 'car' contained in it.

13 In lines 30–32. 'Break' is used literally (in breaking up a car) and metaphorically (in breaking the law).

14 *a* 'Car' is less descriptive than 'banger', which refers to an old unreliable car.
b The use of 'banger' followed by 'hammer' sounds like an echo.

15a *a* line 18 *b* line 7 *c* line 40
d line 27

16a and b
Fast

bolt	escaping from control, frightened
dart	suddenly, nimbly
dash	in a hurry
hare	very fast (like a hare)
rush	in a hurry

Slow

amble	in a leisurely way
creep	quietly to avoid detection
saunter	in a leisurely way
stalk	with long steps in a stately manner
stroll	in a leisurely way
wander	aimlessly

Unit 3

Section 1

1 B

2 A. The use of 'binmen' instead of 'refuse men'.

3

	Conversational
scientist	boffin
taxi-driver	cabbie
bus conductress	clippie
policeman	cop
criminal	crook

4 C focuses on human interest.
   D is written from the scientific angle.

5 C F
   D E

6a In article G, the word 'naked' immediately catches the eye because of the size of the print. Details of who the girl was and where she was found appear in larger print before the mention of the arrest.
   In article H, the arrest is mentioned first in some detail and the print is all the same size, giving the facts more equal weighting.

b G She was naked. She was pretty. She was a groom. She was 18. Her name was Suzanne Thatcher. Her boss was a friend of Prince Philip. Her body was found very close to the Royal horse show. She had been strangled.
   H Her name was Suzanne Elizabeth Thatcher. She was unmarried. She was naked. She came from Bron Manod. She was a groom. She worked for a Swansea family. She was found in Cirencester Park, where her employers were competing in a horse show.

c The writer of article G focuses on the sensational fact that she was naked. He emphasises her royal connections. He reports that she was pretty, a fact which may or may not be relevant to her murder.
   The writer of article H restricts himself more to the essential facts of the case, such as the arrest, where the girl's body was found and why she had been there.

Section 2

1a A
b in jaws of crusher

2 The potential danger the baby was in: A
   The baby's condition now: B

3 B

4a A
b Reference to the baby's size, particularly with a word like 'tiny', encourages a more vivid picture of the helplessness of the child and is likely to arouse sympathy in the reader.

5a The initial sounds of the two words in 'Bin babe' are the same.
b 'Bin babe' is shorter and gives a more dramatic rhythm.

6

	more descriptive
angry	—— furious
cold	—— freezing
dry	—— parched
fat	—— obese
funny	—— hilarious
hot	—— boiling
hungry	—— starving
large	—— enormous
thin	—— skeletal
tired	—— exhausted
wet	—— soaking

Section 3

1a A power failure.

1b and 2

A	B
rooms freezing	rooms freezing
rooms unlit	rooms unlit
no power	no radios etc.
	no fridges
	1 cramped rooms
	2 inadequate cooking facilities
	3 too few bathrooms
	4 mice and rats
	5 overlooks jail

3a Five (see the list above).
b The use of large dots.

4a Perhaps four, five or six hundred.
b Fewer.
c It would give the impression that the writer thought the number of nurses affected was small.

5 Article A states that heating has been restored. Article B states that heating will be restored by New Year's Eve.

6 A D
   B C

7 outrage: B
   sympathy: A

Section 4

1a *1* C
    2 A
    3 B
b To arouse the readers' interest and make them want to find out the full details of what happened by reading on.

2 *a* more *b* less *c* less *d* less
   e more

3a A she had told the tribunal of her 'embarrassment' (line 19)
    B was smiling (line 2); I am very happy (line 9); she was annoyed (lines 12–13)

C blew her top (line 11)
b B

4   It is shorter and more conversational.

5   This is a play on words. She went crackers (lost her temper) and showered the steward with crackers (biscuits).

6   B

7   Drawing attention to the use of a pun. *a*
     Quoting the title of a book etc.   *d*
     Quoting someone else's words.   *b, c*

8   A *a b d g h*
     C *a c d e f h i j*

9   Human interest details.

Section 5

1   Probably about a motorist who gets into serious trouble.

2   *b*

3   *b*

4   *c*

5   *a* is probably the most likely.

6   *a* and *b* are probably the most likely.

7   'Dead' can mean both 'serious' and 'not alive'.

8   No. The facts are perfectly obvious.

9a   'Posthumous' means 'after death'. It is strange to talk of someone collecting something after he is dead.
  b   Humour through irony.

10a Medals or honours for brave actions that led to the person's death.
  b   Humour through irony.

11   *b*

12a *a*
  b   It would seem in very bad taste.

Unit 4

Section 1

1   *b*

2   *b*

3   *a*

4   The judge's pronouncement in lines 23–26.

5   *a*

6   *b*

7   The use of big dots.

8   *1 e 2 d 3 f 4 b 5 c 6 a*

9   *b*

10   *c*

11   And as if all this were not enough (line 78)

12   *a*

13   'which they will' = They will remove it.

14   *c*

15   *c* (*a* According to the writer, the driver has never been king of the road. The headline is, therefore, factually incorrect. *b* suggests that the writer is in favour of the police action. *d* refers to only a small part of the article.)

Section 2

1   They seem a little exaggerated.

3c   The writer hopes to surprise the reader, creating a humorous effect through irony.

4a   Contradictory.
  b   Humour through irony.

5   keeping out draughts

6   'Feeling different' could mean feeling better or worse.

7   *a*

8   The humorous diet should be completed with the following items: piece rope, Shredded Timber, sisal juice, Shredded Timber, sisal, the pack in which the cereal came, newsprint derivative, rope, tarry, wholecord rope

9   Ridiculous.

10   There can be little doubt now that 'different' means worse (see 6 above).

11a The Moreover One-Day Crash Fibre Course is not a solemn, joyless affair (lines 12–14).
  b   The dieter is allowed to chew his fingernails and gnaw his knuckles and his moustache (lines 14–17).
  c   When under stress.

12   This is an understatement. You would expect to be very hungry.

13a He finds it all ridiculous.
  b   *d*

Section 3

1   Emotions.

2a   lines 9–20
  b   cruelty, mutilation, supposed interests

3   in the judgement of the scientists

4   *b*

5   *b*

6   *a*

7   Yet (line 50)

8a *The Plague Dogs*, a novel by Richard Adams.
 b No.

9 *a*

10a The thought of the many thousands of experiments undertaken simply to serve scientific curiosity or, worse, to pamper human beings.
 b He doesn't think it is an important part of scientific progress.

11 *c*

12a *a* false *b* true *c* false *d* true
   e true *f* false *g* true *h* false

13 *c* (*a* The opinion expressed is too mild. *b* The opinion expressed is the opposite to that of the writer. *d* The use of 'the following' indicates that the writer is now going to list the reasons. It would not, therefore, come at the end of an article.)

Section 4

1 Yes. Both articles think the laws should be changed.

2 The Government has withdrawn its support for the change.

3 keep the legal shutters up (lines 10–11)

4a The Bill to reform the laws.
 b The unions, the Sabbatarians and some retail groups.

5 *b*

6 They show that s/he is opposed to the people who do not support the Bill.

7 *a*

8 The battle is on (line 1), crusaded (line 12)

9a An earlier report in the same newspaper.

10 *b*

11a the Sunday killjoy lobby (lines 13–14)
 b killjoy

12 C B ('Sell-out' refers to shopping, on the one hand, and the Government's action, on the other. To 'sell out' means to sell everything. It also means to betray someone.)
   D A ('Service, please' is a phrase used in some shops to attract the attention of the assistant. It is also the writer's call for the Government to serve the people who elected it by following their wishes in this matter.)

13 *a* Very formal phrases e.g. 'let nobody underestimate' (line 6), 'has long crusaded' (line 12).

 b No contractions. Compare 'We shall not relax' (lines 13–14) in article A with 'won't help' (lines 4–5), 'don't bother' (lines 11–12) in article B.

14a No. Neither article explains why the change might be a bad thing.

Section 5

1 *a 3 b 6 d 1 e 5 f 7 g 2 h 8 i 4*

2 *b*

3a *c*
 b *a*

4a a glimpse of the chasm (lines 4–6)
 b the handicapped
 c the people of Teignmouth

5 'herding' (line 23) suggests that the writer feels that this is treating people like cattle.

6 *a* lines 30–33
   b lines 44–49

7a the able-bodied (line 62)
 b restricting the number (line 22)

8 *a* ✗ quite unjustifiably (line 38)
   b ✓ quite rightly (line 53)
   c ✓ sadly (line 63)

9 *b*

10 *a* line 60 – . . . in which they have a place—and in many areas it is working.
   b line 33 – . . . were mentally handicapped—hardly a proportion to flood the town.
   c line 49 – . . . holiday resorts—like wrecking them.
   d line 71 – . . . on a slippery slope—quotas for the handicapped today, restrictions for the elderly tomorrow.

Unit 5

Section 1

1 A Kent Invicta, who are based in Maidstone
   B Fred Winter, who has been the champion trainer seven times
   C A birdie scored at the last hole by American Charlie Bolling
   D Aston Villa's 22-year-old defender Brendan Ormsby, who is seeking a transfer
   E Miss Reeves, who hugs the base-line

2 George Sloan, 42 years old, is an ex-champion amateur jockey. Based in Tennessee, where he is a health spa impressario, he commutes across the Atlantic. Yesterday at Newbury . . .

3 A *a* Southport toppled Walton.
    b This happened last weekend.

c Until then Walton had been league leaders. *d* Southport took over at the top of the table. *e* Southport went to the top on goal difference.

Last weekend Southport toppled Walton from their position as league leaders. Southport now take over at the top on goal difference.

B *a* Cherry defies all golf theory. *b* He drives majestically. *c* He putts devastatingly. *d* His left arm is permanently bent. *e* He had an operation. *f* This was eight weeks ago.

Cherry defies all golf theory. He drives majestically and putts devastatingly although his left arm is now permanently bent following an operation he had eight weeks ago.

C *a* He is ranked No. 1 in Spain. *b* He is ranked eighth in the world. *c* He out-played Jimmy Connors. *d* Jimmy Connors was reigning world champion. *e* He reached the semi-finals of the French Championships. *f* He did this last year.

Jose Higueras is ranked No. 1 in Spain and eighth in the world. Last year he reached the semi-finals of the French Championships by outplaying Jimmy Connors who was at that time the reigning world champion.

D *a* He has enjoyed his best-ever season. *b* He rides under National Hunt rules. *c* He was at Newbury. *d* He saddled Vivaque. *e* He finished second. *f* Ash King won. *g* The race was the Tote Credit Hurdle.

David Elsworth has enjoyed his best-ever season riding under National Hunt rules. At Newbury he saddled Vivaque and finished second to Ash King in the Tote Credit Hurdle.

Section 2

1 *1* A *2* C *3* F *4* B *5* G *6* E
  7 D *8* H

Section 3

1 *c*

2 *a*

3a Fifty Dollars More.
 b Fifty Dollars More.

4 *a* That a five-horse race would be an anti-climax.
  b That Fifty Dollars More would win.

5 goals, records

6 *a* The record for the number of goals scored in a career.
  b 100 goals in 50 games.

7 'But' suggests a contrast. Altrincham did badly, therefore you would expect that Dundee won.

8 Altrincham had won 12 games in a row.
  They had lost two games before they played Cleveland.

9 Dundee.

10 *b*

11 Four.

12 Southampton.

13 'For *consistency* . . . *lost* 15 in a row.'
  Consistency is usually regarded as positive; losing as negative.

Section 4

1
Doncaster Rovers		Worcester	
Wigan Ath.	W	Coventry	W
Halifax T.		Weymouth	
Sheffield Utd.	W	Cambridge	W
Everton	D	Wrexham	
Newport	D	Brentford	W
Shrewsbury	W		
Rotherham			

2 crushed devastated hammered thrashed trounced won by a mile

3 *a* broke the deadlock *b* put __ ahead *c* pulled a goal/one back *d* equalised *e* a hat-trick

4 A 0–2 B 4–1 C 2–0 D 1–2
  E 2–0 F 5–2

5 crashing, drive, slotted (A)
  flick (C)
  bundled (D)
  hammered (E)
  shot (F)

6a and b 'newly promoted' in A means the same as *b*.
  'relegation-haunted' in B means the same as *f*.
  'lowly' in E means the same as *c*.

7 in the dying stages

8 At Wolverhampton—'devastated' is stronger than 'thrashed'.

9 squander a couple of sitters

10 *a* foul *b* caution *c* book *d* send off

11 clout ram rap thud thump

Section 5

1 *a* most devastating *b* vastly superior *c* rapidly widened to embarrassing proportions *d* more flawlessly majestic *e* pounded *f* dazzling.

3 solitary decent shot, drab game, mercifully blew the final whistle, . . . what a
   farce it would have been, to endure,
   absolute nothingness, the most exciting
   moment was when . . . , blessedly,
   unexpectedly good

4 consistent   predictable
   adventurous   reckless
   youthful   inexperienced
   conventional   boring
   individualistic selfish
   casual   careless
   flamboyant   ostentatious

Section 6

1 The loss of a battle; the aftermath of an
   invasion or disaster.

2a S/he takes it very seriously.
 b Because they have lost to Australia.
 c It would seem melodramatic and
    ridiculous.

3 There would be no double meaning.

4 *c*

5 citations, outgunned (headline),
   manoeuvres (line 1), basic training and
   personnel (lines 3–4), heavy infantry
   (line 30), cavalry (line 31)

6 A Ferrari, Chevrolets, blew up their
   engines (motor-racing)
   B Grand National hopefuls, cleared
   . . . fences, fallers, the going gets
   tougher (horse racing)
   C king, claimant to his throne
   (royalty)
   D balance of power, region, seat,
   gains, standing in the polls (political
   elections)
   E go down, becalmed (sea-faring)—
   the reporter also takes advantage of
   the double meaning of 'Bath'.

Section 7

1a *a* B *b* C
 b A—details of the atmosphere, fans,
    colourful action.

2 A E B D C F

3b G *a b f*
    H *a b c d e f g h*

4 *1 a 2 c 3 b*

5a Ron Hill
 b The 50 men who finished inside 2 hours
    16 minutes and 30 seconds.
 c Gratton and Helme

6 *a*

7a and b
        Technical

        b went better by over 4½ minutes

        Mike Gratton, from the Invicta
        Club in Kent

        with his time of 2hr 9min 44
        sec, a personal improvement of
        2 min 22 sec.

        Non-technical

        There were many personal best
        times

        Michael Gratton, from Canterbury

        (Grete Waitz) was 14 minutes
        behind the winner

8 It would be less descriptive and
   colourful.

9a Because it is an article on men's
    athletics.
 b They include non-technical details of
    her physical appearance.

10a K
  b L

11 G N
    H M

12 G People interested in the details of
    men's athletics.
    H People interested in that particular
    marathon from a general point of view
    (the atmosphere, how men and women
    runners compared, main records
    broken etc.).